T0067107

17 Years and Still Struggling

HENRY L. STAMPLEY

authorHOUSE®

AuthorHouse™
1663 Liberty Drive
Bloomington, IN 47403
www.authorhouse.com
Phone: 1 (800) 839-8640

Published by AuthorHouse   04/17/2015

ISBN: 978-1-5049-0763-7 (sc)
ISBN: 978-1-5049-0762-0 (e)

Print information available on the last page.

This book is printed on acid-free paper.

CONTENTS

Dedication vii

New chapter.. 1

New chapter.. 5

New chapter.. 6

The boys--routines.. 7

The boys-bus routines.. 8

The boys-testing/benefits.. 12

Tavarius 20

Demarian... 42

New chapter.. 49

New chapter.. 50

New chapter.. 54

New chapter.. 60

About the Author 63

DEDICATION

I would like to thank my wonderful wife Gwendolyn Stampley for being the remarkable, dedicated and loving wife that she has been through all these years. She has been my rock through this whole journey. And I would also like to thank our Daughter Takisha Stampley Harper for helping me to get through this book project and taking care of business at hand. I also would like to thank the rest of my family members for there support.

In my previous book, I gave you the story of Tavarius and Demarian and the struggles my family endured in our fight for them and their rights. Most of the fighting was played out in the Juvenile Court System. This time around I would like to share with you the unpleasant side of being a foster or adoptive parent. For the most part, my wife and I thought that once the adoptions were final, the struggles would be over. We couldn't have been more wrong. You will find out as we did, that adopting a child out of the system does not end the fight. There are still some things you will have to endure that you should not have to deal with, especially when it comes to children with disabilities. Adoption was a huge roadblock, and we thought that once it was complete everything would fall in place. Sadly that is not the case. There is nightmare after nightmare after nightmare. I have learned to continue praying and to do what I can to make things different. I believe that one day those prayers will be answered and I am trusting and believing God for that. Even if our family doesn't benefit from my fight, I know that down the road, others will. I might not be here for that time, but at least my struggle will not have been in vain.

Our story is not the only story. It's just that most of the other stories haven't been told. There are some that are much worse than ours, but you will never know that if the stories remain untold. There are people who are working for the best interest of the children and want to come forward. They won't come though because they are afraid of retaliation, or even worse, that the children might be removed from their homes. It is a horrible and frightening thing to have children in your home that have been mistreated, children that you love as your own, but you are afraid to come forward and expose the wrongdoings of the system, for fear of losing those children.

NEW CHAPTER

In February of 2008, we had the opportunity to do our very first television interview. It was on one of our local stations and we were very excited, or at least I was. My wife was nervous. To be honest, I was nervous too, but not too nervous to tell our story. I was excited for the opportunity to have our five minutes of fame. This situation we are in has been eating at me for years. Making the appearance was bittersweet. Bitter because the story in the book is really about how horrible things happened that could have been prevented, and the effect these things have had on so many lives-directly and indirectly.

The sweet was we were able to share our story with an audience that may have never known the things that we know about some of the children that are in the foster care system. The fact that there were thousands of people watching this show gave me some joy and satisfaction. At the very least, it meant more people would be educated after our appearance than people who knew beforehand. We silently hoped our appearance would eventually encourage other people to come forward and tell their horror stories. We need to get other people to speak up.

On February 11, 2008 we had the interview. The show was Live at 9 with Marybeth Conley and Alex Coleman. The interview went very well and I would like to thank them for allowing us to share our story. Before we could get home from the interview we were getting messages congratulating us for the outstanding job that we had done speaking on our situation with our children. The overflow of support had us feeling so blessed.

It made us feel wonderful inside to know that people cared. The ease with which we were able to give that interview and the feedback we received just gave me more of an incentive to continue our fight for abused and neglected children. We want to do all we can do to try and prevent others from going through the things we have.

Our local newspaper, the Commercial Appeal, was slated to run an article about my sons, my wife and I on September 20, 2008. On the morning of September 11, I got a phone call from Mr. Sparks at the

Commercial Appeal informing us that they wanted to move the date from the 20th to the 16th. I didn't mind the change, I was just excited about the exposure that it would provide for my sons and other children like them.

The photographer for the story came to our home to take pictures. She actually caught us on the day we normally take the boys to the barber shop. She arrived at the house around 5:20pm and we had to be at the barber shop at 6:30pm. As she was waiting for us to get ready to go, she took pictures of us and asked us if she could tag along for the trip. Even after we told her the drive was about 30 minutes on the other side of town, she still insisted. My wife and I were really moved by her interest in the boys. Particularly because we sensed that it was genuine and that she was going outside of the scope of her duties.

The morning the story appeared, we got a call from our friend Effie letting us know that the article was in the paper. The article was entitled "Couple Finds Room in Their Hearts for Two Boys Who Require Extra Help." Our story covered a whole section. We were pleased with the article and even went to the online version to see if the public was equally impressed. There were 32 comments on the story, one of which was negative. 32 is actually a nice amount considering that most people who still read the paper, read it in print and don't leave comments on line. We appreciated each comment, even the negative one. The fact that the story is still online, continues to help us in our campaign to tell our story because even today, we run into people that tell us how touching our story is.

Receiving attention from the media really helps with our quest to get the word out. But personal relationships are equally as important.

My neighbor actually invited me to her church to speak. I spoke about my first book which detailed a lot of things we went through with the foster care system. After everything was over, they presented us with flowers, a gift card, and a cake with Tavarius' picture on it. The experience was touching.

On one occasion I ran into a former classmate of mine who had heard about my book. When she heard about my book she jumped in with both feet. Joyce was moved by our story and wanted to become involved in our journey to push my book and to increase awareness of our cause. She felt our pain and we felt hers as we shared the dreadful events surrounding the special needs children in our lives. Joyce has been wonderful and very supportive. She has been both an inspiration and a blessing to us. She and

I met periodically to discuss different strategies for our campaign. She even introduced me to an organization called 4streetpositive.

4streetpositive is located in San Bernardino, CA and the director is Terry Boykins. I fondly call him Brother Boykins. He is one of the most caring, passionate men that I have ever had the pleasure of meeting. Brother Boykins is definitely about the business of taking care of children. The organization stands for so many positive things and is a part of multiple initiatives to speak out for our children. When I read all the information on the 4streetpositive site, I couldn't believe all the positive things they were doing for our youth. I was so proud to be affiliated with such an organization.

Brother Boykins and I worked together to create an event that we titled "Push Across Memphis." It would be a collaborative effort between myself and 4streetpositive. Brother Boykins has extremely remarkable marketing skills and was responsible for really making all the right connections. The purpose of the event was to bring awareness to Shaken Baby Syndrome and child abuse and neglect. Despite the fact that he was in California and I in Memphis, we were able to pull it off. There were a few challenges, but overall I was pleased with the outcome.

We put individuals together to form relay teams that would push my son and his wheelchair twenty-two miles across Memphis. Each team was responsible for pushing the wheelchair at least one mile. It didn't matter how they chose to meet that goal, whether they split it up individually or did it collectively, as long as they covered their mile. The "Push" was supposed to begin with me and Brother Boykins pushing Tavarius two miles and then removing him from the chair while the other teams pushed the empty chair for the remaining miles.

The reason we made the decision to remove Tavarius after two miles in the wheelchair was because he had surgery on his hips and we didn't want him to be uncomfortable or agitated. While we were adamant about making a strong statement, we didn't want to do it at the expense of Tavarius. However on the day of the event my adrenaline kicked in after the first two miles and Tavarius still seemed to be enjoying the outside air, so I actually ended up pushing him for five miles.

We started out in the inner city where I grew up and attended church and school. Our mission was to end the 22 miles in the suburbs on the outskirts of Memphis. It was to symbolize us "moving forward." We were on a mission to bring this terrible disease and its cohorts to the forefront.

It ended up raining the day of the event and we didn't get the participation that we were expecting. We did accomplish what we set out to do and prove not just to others but ourselves as well, that even with thousands of miles between us we were able to come together and make it happen. The rain started at our halfway point, but we kept going and we completed our mission with the help of God and the support of people that cared and believed in what we were trying to do. To have been a part of something like that gives me chills every time I think about it. It took us about a year to put the event together which I think was a big accomplishment considering we didn't have the financial or political support to help pull off the event. We did reach out and we didn't ask for any money, just a contribution of time and support to the cause. Unfortunately, we still didn't receive that. We just wanted notable support taking part in something that we knew would be of great importance to people of all walks of life. Child abuse and neglect have no boundaries.

The fact that we couldn't even get their support by presence alone, makes me wonder if our government really has any interest in doing what it will take to try to stamp out abuse. When an event like "Push Across Memphis", is presented to educators, city officials, and politicians without asking for any financial contributions, it seems there should be an overflow of support to bring awareness and education to this issue. Unfortunately that wasn't the case. I even gave copies of my book to individuals that I knew were in a position to help, or at least get the information in the hands of the right people. The only thing I asked in return was for them to let me know what they thought about the book. Not one of those people got back in touch with me. I could have easily given those books to individuals that I know would have been more than happy to take one and read it. I gave away books to individuals that I knew could afford to purchase them, but my goal was to raise awareness, not money. The problem is, I feel that they really had no intentions on reading the book or maybe honestly, didn't have the time. I would have appreciated the honesty though, as opposed to the cold shoulder.

NEW CHAPTER

When you have children with special needs it is such a blessing to have a strong support system. My wife, Gwendolyn Stampley has been my silent partner in all of this. I say silent because I am normally the one with the "voice" about things that are going on, but her role in taking care of the boys is equal to mine. This is a team effort. I have so much gratitude for her, the things she's done, and the things that she has sacrificed in order to take care of these boys. I certainly would not have been able to endure this journey alone. A lot of times when my wife would come home from work, I knew that she was tired but she was never too tired to help me out with the boys and I have never heard her complain. Although I was the one home with the boys all day, when Gwen would come home from work she would immediately dive in to help. I used to try to let her relax, but she would insist on doing something. She plays the background role but she is definitely a dedicated advocate for the boys.

Saturdays are normally her days to pamper herself. I remember distinctly one Saturday I wasn't feeling well. She got up earlier than normal, woke the boys and cleaned them up. She then went to the store, came back and fed them—all of this before going to the beauty shop. It was important to her that the boys were taken care of and she didn't mind making that sacrifice so that I could have less to do. It is the small things like that which make me appreciate her. I know a few women who would not be late for a hair appointment, regardless of what else may have been going on at the time. In addition to taking care of the boys, she still finds the time to spend with our grandchildren. We are a normal family with ups and downs just like everyone else, but we definitely have our priorities in place. The first of course, being God—without Him none of this would be possible. Then come Tavarius and Demarian. Anyone who knows us knows that those boys are our life. Despite the many sacrifices we have made to take care of them, we have no complaints. And it makes things a lot easier when you deal with difficult situations and there are two of you and you are both on the same page.

NEW CHAPTER

When unexpected things happen we have to come up with a plan for Tavarius and Demarian. Unfortunately it is never as simple as getting them dressed and walking out the door. Regardless of what is going on around us, our sons need 24-hour care and if something comes up we have to make allowances for that. My best friend's mother passed a few years ago. The day we got the phone call it was actually the day of my daughter's baby shower. I tried to remain in good spirits, but that phone call made it very difficult. It is always a tragedy to lose someone that you love, especially your parents. I lost both of mine so I knew what he was going through and how as a friend, it was important for me to be there for him.

The day before the funeral, wanting to be supportive during the wake, I had to pay someone to watch the boys until my wife got home from work. That's not our most ideal situation but those are our babies and we do what we have to do. At the time my daughter was nine-months pregnant and due any day. But on the day of the funeral we asked her for her help. I am so grateful that our children have been supportive and understanding with their disabled brothers. We weren't going to be out for a long time, the fire station was right up the street, and of course if something happened she could have called 911. But the fact that she was even willing to put herself in that situation for us and her brothers spoke volumes. We really appreciated that.

On rare occasions we have the opportunity to travel. And for a family like us it requires more planning than usual. One year we decided to attend a family reunion. Because the boys would not be traveling with us we also had to plan for their care. Although we were looking forward to the much needed vacation, we knew we had to be selective about who would be keeping the children. Our children require a lot of attention, and Demarian has to be watched constantly. We would have loved to take them with us but their medical circumstances would have made that an extremely difficult and uncomfortable feat. Outside of the fact that we would be staying in a hotel, some of their food has to be prepared a certain way. Not to mention that because of their conditions, they can both be extremely noisy at times—screaming and hollering noisy.

THE BOYS--ROUTINES

Dealing with the court system definitely took a toll on our family, but more grueling than that are the routines that we have to go through each day for both of our boys. Each morning our routine begins at 6:00 am. My wife and I wash the boys up, change them, brush their teeth and hair, get them dressed and then give them their medication. Their buses come early enough and deliver them to school on time so that they can eat breakfast at school. Every day, despite what is going on I also have to make sure that I am home by the time Tavarius and Demarian arrive home from school so that I can get them off the school bus. The children arrive home at different times. Demarian normally arrives home at 3:30pm. Once I get him off the bus, I change him, feed him and then wait for Tavarius. Tavarius normally arrives home around 4:00pm. Once he arrives I follow the same routine with him. Thankfully, Tavarius has an aide that comes in three times a week. She is great with him, and when she is present, she takes over my afternoon routine for him and even gives him his bath. By the time my wife arrives home from work it is time for Demarian (and Tavarius when his aide isn't present) to have their last dose of medication and baths. Tavarius takes medication three times a day and Demarian takes it twice a day, both seven days a week. By 8:30pm the routine is complete and we have put them both to bed.

That is the routine that we basically follow seven days a week. The only difference being on the weekends, when we don't wake them up as early and there is no school. But even on the weekends, we have to make sure that Demarian is fed first because he is used to that routine. He gets restless if we do it any other way. I think his thought process is if Tavarius eats first, there will be nothing left for him. With the condition that Demarian has, whenever he sees food he wants to eat. His brain doesn't tell him when he is full. We have to monitor his intake and know when he has had enough to eat.

THE BOYS-BUS ROUTINES

Believe it or not schooling also poses an issue when you have children with disabilities. There was a time when Tavarius and Demarian attended the same school. Things were easier then. As they got older, they were assigned to different schools because of their different disabilities. Tavarius actually maxed out at the school he had attended for eight years. We really hated that. With the new assignment of schools came our new responsibility of learning the systems of each of their schools and making sure that each child's special needs were met at their respective schools. These tasks are important not only inside of the schools but with their transportation as well.

That is why it is important to be a strong advocate for your children, especially when they have special needs. Changing schools is like uprooting them from one place and starting all over again in another. Maybe the transitions would be easier if they didn't have special needs. We are just very protective of our children. People that have special needs children deal with a lot. You almost have to be in a situation like this, to know exactly what I am talking about.

Both of our children are transported to and from school on the school bus. It is essential to get to know their bus drivers and their schedules. There is a set time for them to be picked up. So we have to make sure the boys are picked up in the mornings and dropped off in the evenings when they should be. Believe it or not, it's not an easy task. Some people do just enough to do their "job." But there are others who will go the extra mile. Tavarius had the same driver for about seven years and when the boys attended the same school she drove for both of them. Although it was a rare occasion, she would let us know if she was going to be late picking them up or dropping them off. We really appreciated her and her regard for our children made her very special to us. There is nothing like having that open line of communication with the people who are taking care of your children. Having to create that again with all new people was a daunting but necessary task. Hopefully we will continue to foster great relationships. For years we were blessed to have a driver and teachers that went the extra mile, and didn't mind doing it. It makes a difference when you know that the people taking care of your children have their best interest in mind.

When he had a different driver once Demarian's bus was about 30 minutes late bringing him home. No one called us to inform us that the bus would be late. I had to call them. It was only after the bus arrived at our home that I was informed by the driver of the reason they were late. It was because another child had been added to the route. Well of course I don't have a problem with another child being added to the route. What I do have a problem with is not being informed about this situation in a timely manner. My concern was that I was waiting for my child to return home at a specific time and that didn't happen, nor did anyone inform me of any changes.

On another occasion Demarian was picked up 40 minutes late. Once again, no one called. Then when I called, the only thing they said was that the bus had broken down and that it would be another 40 minutes before the bus would arrive. Don't get me wrong, I'm not nitpicking because we know better than anyone that anything could happen or go wrong at any given moment. But it wouldn't have taken much for them to call us and inform us that the bus would be late. It's about being considerate. If our children are not going to school the following day, then we inform the driver that they will not be going so that no time is wasted driving to our house, only to find out they made a blank trip. If something happens after school hours and we know they won't go the next day, we call early that morning to inform them of the absence instead of waiting until the driver arrives and then letting them know. That would be inconsiderate on our part. We would only like the same consideration in return.

Let's just say that at the beginning of the school year, you had just gotten the job that you had worked so hard to get—a job that comes around maybe once in a lifetime. Let's say that job depended on you to be on time every day. Well, most jobs require you to be on time. So let's say that your job required you to deal with people's lives every day—like a 911 operator, a policeman, fireman, or even a school crossing guard. A life can be lost or saved in a matter of moments. If people in these particular professions don't make it to work on time, it could easily have a bearing on someone's life.

You may say that I am overreacting but think about it. Say that the police department is already shorthanded and you call in a couple of times a week stating that you will be late because the school bus hasn't picked up your child. The crime doesn't stop. Here's another one for you. You're a fireman or a paramedic and you call the station and tell them that you will be late because your child's school bus was late. Once again, your station is already short-handed and at the last minute, they don't have anyone to fill in for you. These things do happen, maybe not all the time. But they do happen. What if this happened with the school crossing guard? What about the 911 operator? Do you know how many children's lives depend on them?

If any of the above scenarios took place, how long do you think that job would be there for you? As harsh as it may seem, the world doesn't work like that. Some people may even suggest that I take them to school. With special needs children it really isn't that simple. A lot of these children are wheelchair bound and a lot of parents don't have vans with lifts on them. All I am asking is to communicate with the parents that depend on you and your services. If the driver is going to be late and you know this in advance, then call the parent. Don't wait until you get there late and say they added another child to the route or the bus broke down. It's not like there are 20-30 phone calls that need to be made. The most amount of children I have seen on the bus is four or five.

Then, as if we weren't already having a difficult time, at one point, the school system decided to change some of the bus routes. And of course, some of those changes involved the routes of special needs children. Here we go again. In the past, the school buses would drop the children off at a designated location (home or otherwise) that was agreed upon between the parents and the school. They allowed this arrangement because of working parents and their schedules. A lot of the parents are at work during the time that the children are either picked up or dropped off. In those cases they were permitted to make other arrangements. This allowance was made because of the special needs of the children. But now, the school board is saying the children can only be picked up or dropped off at their place of residence. What a shame. Politics and money rule the world.

The following school year, the school system changed the company that ran and operated the bus system. Unfortunately, the results were the same. The buses are still late picking up the children and there are still faulty mechanical problems with the buses. We were also told along with the new transportation system would come new buses. The buses looked new but they operated more like refurbished buses. I understand that even new vehicles break down but it was too much. If the buses did that and school had just started, imagine what the rest of the school year was like. Over the years, I have vented my frustration to the school, the transportation service, and even the Board of Education. I can honestly say that I have gotten great and concerned responses from the school and the Board of Education. Unfortunately the transportation service seems to show little or no concern at all.

The seatbelt standpoint on the buses also bothers me. Every driver and their passengers have to have seatbelts on while in a vehicle. But for some reason when it comes to children riding on these school buses the seatbelt law isn't enforced. Everyone talks about the youth of today and how important they are. But somehow when it comes to their safety the importance of things always seems to be about the dollar. How can you put a dollar sign on a child's life? Something is terribly wrong with this picture.

Ever since Tavarius and Demarian have been in our home there has always been a battle when it comes to their well-being. We have battles dealing with the Department of Children services to the Department of Transportation to the insurance companies regarding their services and medication. It is definitely an uphill battle and extremely tiring, but we know that God is in control and that we are trying to do the right thing for these children.

THE BOYS-TESTING/BENEFITS

Outside of the daily routines we have for each of them, we have other routines and activities that we have to be consistent with to ensure that our boys are continuously monitored medically and that they receive all of the benefits to which they are entitled. Some of the processes that we have to go through to secure this assistance seem unreasonable.

For example, both of the boys have to have the Tennessee-Comprehensive Assessment Program test administered to them at school. This makes no sense to us at all and we have no idea what will be accomplished by them taking the test.

There is also a local agency that provides funding for the boys once a year. My wife and I received a disturbing call from the agency informing us that Tavarius and Demarian needed to have a physiological evaluation and that their IQs needed to be below 70 in order for them to receive the funds. With their medical conditions, how could their IQ *not* be below 70? To say we were angry would be putting it mildly. Neither of the boys is self-sufficient in any manner and they both attend schools for the medically fragile. According to doctors, their conditions are not expected to improve at any time during their lifetime. In fact, they are expected to get worse. We didn't understand the phone call because it is clearly evident that the boys qualified for the assistance. Even though we knew this was an unnecessary obstacle, we obliged without argument, because we knew it would work out in favor of our boys. But it was an unjustified and questionable request. I almost think it was some sort of backlash from my first book.

Both of our sons have multiple disabilities that have been well documented so it makes no sense to have to evaluate them annually. I'm not even sure how you would test a child's IQ that cannot read, write, speak, or comprehend. We found out that Tavarius had an IQ of 20 and Demarian's was 45. We didn't know exactly what the numbers would be, but we weren't surprised that they were low. We expected that.

Tavarius was 11 at the time and most of his tests indicated that he functions on the level of a one year old. When he was tested on his fine motor skills, the test indicated that he functioned on the level of a five-month old. On his self-help test, he functioned on the level of a 14 -month old. On social skills, he functioned on the level of a six-month old and on communication skills, the level of a nine-month old.

On one of Demarian's tests, he scored a zero. He wasn't able to point to any items that were stacked or shapes of things to make a pattern. He wasn't able to mimic hand movements. He wasn't able to stack any of the items on top of each other with any degree of accuracy. He did not appear to understand the concept of pointing and selecting an answer. Demarian also had great difficulty holding a pencil in either his right or left hand. His results of the psycho educational assessment indicated that his intellectual functioning fell within the extremely low range compared to other children the same age. The test stated that Demarian met the Tennessee eligibility criteria for mental retardation and orthopedic impairments.

Yet with these results we are still expected to have them tested annually when none of their handicaps are expected to improve. Although Demarian was born with his condition, Tavarius was not. I wonder if aggressors of crimes like the one committed against him have to be physiologically tested every year. I'm sure they don't. For children like Tavarius and Demarian who are still in the system, I believe their needs would be better served if more energy were given to them receiving the proper care. Then perhaps they wouldn't remain in the system for so long.

Every year the boys have to have their blood drawn just to check the status of their conditions. I understand that, but what I can't understand is why it is that every year we have to have these children's doctors fill out paperwork regarding their condition, especially when the children have lifelong illnesses and conditions. The state tells you that if you do not comply that they will reduce the amount of funds that they give you. I can see that being the case if they think the child's condition might improve. But when you all know the children will be in that state for the rest of their lives, then they shouldn't have to go through this and neither should we. I sincerely believe that one of the reasons that some people don't choose to be foster parents or adopt children is because there is so much unnecessary red tape to deal with. Too much time is spent on needless testing and procedures. I also believe that some of the people that take these children into their homes, are put through more than some of the parents that have abused and neglected these children. I have no idea why, but I also believe that some of the case workers try intentionally to make it hard for us.

Don't get me wrong, you have good case workers that are dedicated and invested in what they do. But you also have those who are going to work just to get a check. I know because we have dealt with both kinds. On the flip side of that, you also have good parents and bad parents, even with the foster parents. When you are dealing with the elements of bad case workers and bad parents, it makes it harder on everyone. All parents shouldn't have to suffer because of the bad parents, but most of the time that's exactly what happens. The case workers shouldn't be able to choose who the rules apply to and who they don't-the same rules should apply for everyone.

Our sons have been living with us respectively for seventeen and twelve years. To a certain degree that doesn't even matter because we still have to submit three different forms of identification on the both of them showing that they still reside in our home. We all know that if they *weren't* living in our home that would be a red flag if nothing else. It just bothers us that the system is not operating as it should be.

Insurance companies don't want to play their part in making sure these children get what they need. Most of their decisions regarding these children, have to deal with how they can save as much money as possible. Tavarius' insurance company was about to change his primary care physician. He had been seeing this physician since he was an infant. When I called to question why the change was being made, they told me it was because the doctor was no longer in their network. After doing my own research, I found that not to be true. Because this doctor knew Tavarius and his conditions very well, we were always given information on how and what to ask for when it came to his care. I believe the insurance company felt if they placed him with another physician, he wouldn't receive the same quality of care and they wouldn't have to process so many accommodations regarding his care. It seems that insurance companies are trying to limit the services that children receive. They believe that if a child doesn't meet their expectations, then the child doesn't need the services. I beg to differ. For anyone confined to a wheelchair, if they don't get any exercise they will become stiff and their muscles will tighten up on them. This can actually be very painful. Therapy and exercise definitely assist with this. Also, if this person is not getting exercise or having any type of physical activity it causes problems with their bowel movements. Irregular bowel movements can create an entirely different set of issues all on their own. We have all been constipated before and it is not a good feeling. Imagine how that would feel on a regular basis. That would be a horrible situation to eat three meals a day, seven days a week, not having a bowel movement, and then not being able to communicate that you are uncomfortable or in pain. I have seen Tavarius this way and it is painful to watch. Although I know what it feels like, it hurts me that he cannot tell me how he feels. I have to watch for certain behavior from him to know that is what he is experiencing. He can't communicate orally what his needs are, so we have to watch for the signs he gives us. When you have been around a child with special needs for a while, you learn their different ways of expression. For example, when he's constipated, he spits his food out. Graciously, he has been prescribed medicine for that so when we see the signs, we try to make sure he's not uncomfortable for too long. Once the medication kicks in, he takes off running—literally. When this happens, we usually end up giving him a bath like three or four times a day.

During one of Tavarius' IEP meetings, we were told that because the therapist felt he would never walk, the therapy sessions we requested would not benefit him. This decision came after he received about nine or ten sessions in our home. And although the therapist was responsible for working with Tavarius during that time, we noticed the therapist was trying to teach the aides some of the routines so they wouldn't have to do it. That's what the therapist was trained and paid to do. How can you make an aide responsible for a fragile child during exercises like that if they are not properly trained? Of course when they made the decision to stop the sessions we were not happy. If he was receiving the therapy on a regular basis, maybe it would have alleviated some of his other ailments. It certainly wouldn't have hurt him. I don't think this was about what was best for Tavarius, but what was best for their budget. The therapy really did help him. I could work with him but not like a trained therapist. There is also the possibility that in trying to work with him that I could seriously injure him so that was definitely not an option.

On one occasion they withheld funds from us because something wasn't written correctly on the paperwork they received from the doctor. We only found out that was the issue after we inquired about it. Even after our inquiry, they waited until the last minute to respond. I felt like they knew they were not giving us enough time to have the corrections made. Instead of them notifying us when they received the paperwork that something wasn't correct, they withheld the funds. We also lost some funds for the children once because paperwork was not submitted on time. The paperwork was actually completed and submitted by the agency. It wasn't our fault, but it certainly wasn't the agency that paid for that mishap. I don't see how any of this benefits the children. It just doesn't seem fair and it doesn't seem as though they are working in the child's best interest. It's not like we don't have enough to go through. Things like that just seem cruel.

These types of requests substantiate the fact that these children need advocates because they are unable to speak for themselves. They are basically helpless and need people to fight for them until the necessary changes regarding their care are made.

We are part of the small percentage that is trying to do right and make a difference in the lives of abused and neglected children's lives. We are trying to be their voice but it seems as though no one is listening. It seems as though paperwork is the priority. It is more important to cross the T's and dot the i's than it is to administer the proper medication and get the children to their doctor's appointments. I would think the children's health would be more important. Before we adopted the children and their parents' rights were terminated, the parents would continuously miss visits and doctor's appointments that they were supposed to attend. The system did nothing but continue to give them chance after chance after chance. This is a clear indication that the priority was not the well-being of these children.

One day I had another parent from Tavarius' school call me and ask me to attend an IEP meeting with her. An IEP is an Individual Education Plan that is normally created for children with special needs to detail their educational goals and progress. If you have never been to one of these meetings before they can be quite intimidating, especially when you do not have a clue about what is going on. For a couple of years I had representation from someone else, so I understood completely what this parent was going through. When it comes to children with special needs a lot of times the staff will play word games with you and if you don't really know what is going on, your child can be left without services that they really need. These meetings can get very heated at times. Sometimes they don't want to provide your child with the services. Sometimes it's about money and sometimes it's about power. I have experienced it before.

While I was in the IEP meeting, I started having flashbacks of my experience. I could see the look of disgust on the parent's face. I was thinking to myself that I was glad she asked me to attend with her. No one should have to experience anything like this without moral support. On top of that, this was a single middle-aged parent who had adopted a child with special needs. She deserved a break…and some passion. At the end of the meeting as we were leaving, one of the individuals on the board told the parent, "Don't bring Mr. Stampley back." Although she had a smirk on her face when she said it, I knew she meant it. That also let me know that I had done what God had sent me there to do and that was fight for this woman and her child.

I just do not believe that our system is operating as it should be and that the children's well-being is a priority. I also don't understand why there aren't more people that are bothered by this shaky system. I understand that there are a lot of people who are not fully educated about the issues, but I also understand that there are a lot of people who are and refuse to speak. If you know what is going on and you turn a deaf ear, then you should feel some sort of guilt or responsibility to step in and do your part. We aren't talking about running a red light or a stop sign. We are talking about innocent children's lives. I'm sure there are a lot of people saying that they hate I became a foster parent because I like to address the issues. But I am also sure there are a lot of people who are glad I became a foster parent and that I have decided to not only speak up on behalf of the children but to share this information with other people. When I no longer walk this earth, I want people to remember that I did what I could to try to make a difference in the lives of children. I want them to know I tried to be a voice those children didn't have. Until that day comes though, I will keep talking and talking until I am heard. I tell our story to anyone who will listen in the hopes that they will share it with someone else. Maybe through these interactions, the story will fall on the right ears of individuals who are capable and compelled to do something to change how things are done.

Something that continues to bother me and weighs heavily on my heart is what will happen to our two sons if I leave this earth before my wife does. I think about it all the time now because the harsh reality of the situation is that it could happen. It could be next year, next month, next week, or even today. For all of these years our plates have been full taking care of Tavarius and Demarian. As we get older and somewhat weaker, they are getting older and stronger. If Gwen had to do it all alone, I know that there would be some tough and hard decisions for her to make. Although I know without a shadow of a doubt that she would continue to love and care for them, the reality is that she might not be able to handle it physically and mentally. Now don't get me wrong, Gwen is an awesome, incredibly strong woman-physically, spiritually and mentally, but taking care of our two special needs sons without the proper help would be devastating. The challenge for her would be unbearable and I know that it would completely break her down. Fifteen or twenty years ago I probably wouldn't have said anything about me leaving here first, or even thought about it, but that is the reality of our situation.

Sure we have family members and we have other children but Tavarius and Demarian are not their responsibility. Although I have played this in my head so many times, it never occurred to me to even ask them if they would consider taking on this responsibility. It was my wife and I that made the decision to become foster parents and then later, parents to our sons. It would not be fair to ask any of them to give up their lives for something that my wife and I chose to do. Now if the conversation comes up and the children say that is something they would want to do, then by all means I would be supportive. I would thoroughly explain to them though, everything that is required to take care of the boys. Yes, they have been around us and the boys to know and see what we do on a daily basis, but there are other duties that come along with that as well. Things such as keeping up with their doctor appointments and giving them their medication properly and at the correct times. There is also the task of investigating when something is ailing them because of course, neither of them can tell you that.

Tavarius turned 17 last year and Demarian turned 12. My wife will be 65 this year and I will be 63. With that we should definitely be thinking about a solution regarding the future of our situation. If our lives take the same direction that my mind has been going in, then we definitely need a good back up plan. It would have to be one that if ever my wife or I are to the point where we are unable to care for our sons, that we will still be able to have some piece of mind about their care. Unfortunately one of the alternatives we may have to explore is institutionalization. Just thinking about that makes me terribly sad and gives me headaches. I have heard so many horror stories about what happens to individuals that end up in nursing facilities or institutions. I have heard everything from people being left to lay in their own feces to being severely abused. Sadly, I know that the day will have to come, but I pray that when God calls either of us home that we already have a solid plan in place that would at least give our boys loving, comfortable, and dedicated surroundings.

It would surely help if I knew for sure that they would at least be loved and cared for in the same manner that we have provided. I know there is no guarantee that other people would treat them the say way we do, but I will continue to pray and ask God for his guidance in putting something in place to make sure that they at least have a chance at that.

TAVARIUS

I have explained to you some of the hardships that my wife and I experience dealing with the system as it relates to our children, and I would also like to share some of the hurdles we have with their illnesses. We were told at an early age that Tavarius would always be a vegetable but he does communicate and on occasion it is verbal. He picked up a new saying- "Stop T." We call him T and he will normally say this when he does something that he shouldn't be doing. Things like screaming or bumping his head against the back of his wheelchair. He is really repeating what he hears because that is what we say to him when we see him doing those things. But it is an indication that his brain is functioning more than they predicted.

Sometimes after his last meal, I put Tavarius in a medical device called a stander. This equipment is used to stretch his muscles. Because he doesn't get a lot of physical activity, this is very important for him and helps to keep him from being stiff. He remains in the stander for 20 to 30 minutes. He has one at school as well. Although this device helps him, it has its disadvantages as well. His therapist at school sent us a letter saying that he wasn't tolerating his exercises. The letter also stated that his hip appeared to be out of place. Doctors had informed us years ago, that as he got older and continued to grow that it could happen. When pressure is put on his legs, it puts pressure on his hips, especially when he is in the stander.

Of course I needed to take him to the doctor regarding the therapist's concerns, but even that becomes an undesirable chore when you are dealing with the transportation services. On the day that he had his appointment, the transportation service did not pick us up until 915a. They were supposed to be there at 845a because Tavarius' appointment was at 930a. Their tardiness added to my frustration because when we go for these appointments we already have to spend two to three hours in the office. I certainly didn't want to add to that time by being late. Normally when we go to the doctor appointments, I will pack Tavarius dry cereal that he likes, mostly Frosted Flakes or Cheerios, because I know we are going to be there for quite a while.

Unless it's an emergency, it really doesn't matter why we need to see the doctor, we are still in for a lengthy visit. We had an appointment once just to get x-rays of his hips. We had an appointment, but at this particular clinic they normally set everyone's appointment at the same time. It's almost like a first come first serve. Just to get x-rays, we were there for two and a half hours.

Since the last transportation service had us over an hour late for Tavarius' doctor's appointment, the next time I tried a different service. Unfortunately it was another bad experience. This was actually the fourth or fifth different service that we had tried. We had an appointment at 930a. The transportation service called us at 630a that morning to let us know they would be at our house between 8a and 830a. I had to call them twice and by 9a they still had not shown up. I had to load the wheelchair and transport Tavarius myself. One of the reasons that I use the transportation service is that parking is limited. I also prefer the service because Tavarius' insurance pays for it and it saves my back. Because of the limited parking I had to roll him in his wheelchair for a block and a half and I also had to put money in a parking meter. Not to mention the fact that we were already running late due to the absent transportation service. Some things you just have to do yourself. I made a decision that day that going forward, I would transport Tavarius to his appointments.

Between Tavarius, Demarian, and myself, sometimes our schedule can get pretty hectic when everyone has doctor's appointments. Although I keep an appointment book for us, I have gone to a couple of doctor visits on the wrong day.

Shortly after I received the letter from his school therapist, Tavarius' hip starting bothering him again. More than it had been in the past. At that time I had no idea what we were going to do. I was pretty sure though that surgery was not an option. As a matter of fact, that recommendation came from his doctors. They said that they would not even consider it unless his hip came completely out of the socket or that it got to the point where he was in constant pain. Every time things like this happen, I get so upset because this is a result of something that didn't have to happen. Something that shouldn't have happened.

After another set of x-rays, we sadly found out that his hip was almost completely out of the socket.

I needed to figure out a way to deal with this anger in me regarding Tavarius' hip. The skin on his hip began to break. It looked like it was peeling, but you could see down to the pink meat. I know that sounds raw, but so is this situation. Every time I look at his hip it makes my blood boil. He is going through this as a result of the abuse he endured. These things just make tears roll down my face. I wish that I could take his pain myself, but unfortunately it doesn't work like that. If it did, he certainly wouldn't have any pain because I would bear all of it; with no hesitation.

One Monday I went to Tavarius' school to watch him swim. That is the day he gets in the swimming pool. It was definitely a joyful experience watching him in the pool. I think being in the pool eases some of the discomfort from his hip and it has also made a major difference with the stiffness in his legs. It doesn't seem to bother him as much since he has been getting in the pool. That is a plus because it seems the pain is more tolerable. I must admit at first Gwen and I were skeptical about him getting in the pool. But once we saw what the teachers did with the children and how they handled them, we were very at ease. The first couple of times I stayed there from the time that he got in until they took him out. In fact both times, I was the one who put his trunks on and carried him to the pool. I am much more comfortable now and only stop in from time to time. It's probably more for me than Tavarius.

Tavarius used to sit in my lap when he got a haircut. Each week that I took him to the barbershop he seemed to be getting a little heavier. I needed to make some sort of adjustment. I wasn't sure what kind, but changes definitely had to be made. I'm not in the best medical health so I knew that as I continued to get older, and Tavarius got older and heavier, we were going to need a plan to make sure that he kept getting to the barbershop. Of course the plan consisted of Tavarius no longer sitting in my lap like he used to do. Now when we get to the barbershop, we put him in his wheelchair and his barber cuts his hair from there. Our barber Keith Moss is so good to us and we appreciate him for that. He actually moves his barber chair out of its original spot and then rolls Tavarius to that same spot and cuts his hair. When he is finished, he has to move his barber chair back to its original spot so that he can continue to cut his other clients' hair. How special is that? Thank you Keith.

Looking at Tavarius, it hurts me so bad because he is blind and confined to a wheelchair all because someone wanted to hurt him instead of love him.

In August of 2008, Tavarius had a major seizure. I had to call 911 I was so terrified. In the past I have seen him have minor seizures. Well, I won't say minor seizures because none of them are minor, but I had never seen him have one like that. In the 12 years that Tavarius had been with us, I had never seen him have a seizure of that magnitude. He had been home from school no more than 30 minutes. I had just changed him and put him back in his wheelchair. When I came out of the bathroom and turned the corner, what I saw nearly scared me to death. Tavarius' body jerked so hard he moved his wheelchair. His eyes rolled back in his head, he drooled, his teeth chattered and he was made this strange noise.

When I called 911, they told me not to give him CPR and to let the seizure run its course. Even though it went on for about two or three minutes, it seemed like forever. I was told that some seizures can last up to ten minutes or longer. By the time the paramedics arrived, the seizure had stopped. They transported him to the hospital and about an hour and a half later he had another one. This time my wife was there. She was on her way home from work and didn't see him have the first one. When she saw him having the seizure, she looked as though she had seen a ghost. She later told me that it looked like something out of a horror movie, and I had to agree.

To see your child lying on a cart in the ER of a hospital is pretty scary, especially if he already has health issues and you don't know what is going on. They gave Tavarius an IV in his arm, and we stayed there about five hours while the medicine ran its course. They then sent us home and told us to follow up with his neurologist. After seeing him like that, I couldn't believe they were sending us home. I was expecting to at least be there overnight.

We later learned that the type of seizure Tavarius had that day was called a Grand Mal seizure. Some people call them violent seizures. We had a friend of ours to tell us that she knew a guy that had a Grand Mal seizure and that it was so violent they called homicide because they thought someone had killed him. When we went to see the neurologist he made the decision to increase the dosage on the medication Tavarius was taking. He had been taking the same dosage since he was an infant. Now that he was older and bigger he needed a larger dosage. After a couple of weeks without another episode, we were convinced that changing his dosage was the right solution.

But just when we thought we were getting the seizures under control, we received a call from one of the nurses at Tavarius' school. She wanted to let us know that Tavarius had had a couple of seizures. Tavarius' history with seizures actually dates all the way back to when he was two months old. They are sadly a result of his shaken baby syndrome. Even though he had a history of seizures we weren't really prepared for her call because it had been a while since he had had one. It was even more alarming because she said he had two—even though they both only lasted a few seconds. I acknowledged the information she gave me and asked her to give me a call if he had another one. She informed me that not only would she give me a call back but she would call 911 as well. They didn't want to take any chances with that situation and of course we didn't either especially since Tavarius had a history. Not to mention the fact that seizures can also lead to death depending on the severity—whether it's one or multiple seizures. Sadly, I got that phone call. Tavarius' nurse called to let me know that he had about 12 seizures back to back and that they had called 911. I let her know that I was on my way to the school. There were so many things going through my mind and I tried to remain calm. It was hard to do that knowing that my child's life was in danger and not knowing what the outcome would be.

On a normal day it would usually take me twenty or twenty-five minutes to get to Tavarius' school. That day it only took me ten to fifteen minutes. When I got to the school the ambulance was already there. Before they put him inside, I witnessed Tavarius having back to back seizures and that scared the hell out of me. Out of all the years that Tavarius had been in our care, he had never experienced that many seizures at one time. I was later told by the nurse that from the time they initially called me until the ambulance got there that he had about twenty-something seizures. Upon arriving at the hospital they admitted him and immediately starting giving him numerous tests trying to figure out why his seizures had spiraled out of control. After all the tests and monitoring him overnight, what they discovered was that Tavarius was going through puberty. Yes puberty, and as a result of that they concluded it was time to change his medication. He had been on the same medication for a number of years. Initially my wife and I were wondering why they wouldn't just change his medication if they knew he would eventually grow out of it. But then we thought about that old saying, "If it ain't broke, don't fix it." If the medicine was still working and wasn't causing any problems, what reason would they have to change it? Watching Tavarius go through something like that was painful and inexplicable. We couldn't figure out what was going on because he had never experienced anything like that before and it was on an entirely different level. Even knowing God as we do and knowing that he can do all things, when something like that happens I just believe it is human instinct to respond in panic mode.

After being educated about the medication he was on and how it affected him, things began to make sense. As he got older some of his medication was no longer as effective as it had been and as a result the seizures kicked into overdrive. After meetings, tests, and comparing notes his doctors decided to change his medicine again. After a few more days in the hospital the new medication seemed to be working and we took Tavarius home. After we got him home we continued to watch him until we felt totally comfortable with the new medication he was on.

I have read where there are some children that have conditions like Tavarius and they will sometimes experience more than 100 seizures a day. I know those parents and caretakers have had some moments where they didn't know if they were coming or going. Those are some very difficult and agonizing moments. Having to take care of children like ours is a 24/7 job. With them you have to always be on alert. They can be fine in the morning and then without any warning things can spin completely out of control.

I will never forget the day. It was Feb 2, a Tuesday morning. I got up to get Tavarius ready for school. But this particular morning something was wrong. As I picked up Tavarius he let out a scream that he would only make if something was hurting him. And something was terribly wrong, I knew it had to be his hips. No matter how I tried to move him, he still screamed. After Gwen and I moved him around and touched him in different areas, we were certain that the agony he was in was being caused by the pain in his hips. Everywhere we touched seem to hurt. We knew it was time to take a trip to the emergency room.

We arrived at the hospital around 8a and they put us in a room around 1030a. After the doctors examined Tavarius they gave him something for pain and they also gave him something for the fever he had contracted. The room that they initially put us in was a room within the emergency facility. Later he was transferred to a permanent room located in another area of the hospital. We knew that meant he would be there for a while. We didn't know how long and it really didn't matter, as long as they were able to find out what was really going on with him and correct the problem. I didn't care how long it took. I was there for the duration.

After they put Tavarius in his room, he was still in a lot of pain but not as much as when we first brought him in. They had given him some pretty strong pain medicine. That first night, the staff was in and out of his room the entire night, and I was awake. Even though he was in the hospital where they had professional doctors and nurses, I could not go to sleep knowing what my child was going through. The next morning they came for Tavarius and took him to have an MRI. The MRI showed that fluid had built up around his hips and around his muscles. After he came back to his room he was cranky and still in some pain. He would not eat anything and the fever that he had kept going up and down.

The more that I looked at Tavarius and saw what he was going through the angrier I would get. If you don't know why I will tell you and if you do know why I will still tell you. I know that I have repeated this over and over again, but I want this to be a constant reminder to everyone how much our child has suffered because someone abused him. I want you to just imagine what this would feel like to you if someone had abused a loved one of yours. Not to mention what the child goes through on a daily basis.

When the weekend came, we were still in the hospital. It was Super Bowl weekend and everyone was talking about the Super Bowl. I am a huge football fan but at that time I could have cared less about a Super Bowl or anything else super unless it was Super wellness to get my child well and out of the hospital. That would be our Super Bowl with Jesus being the winner for getting Tavarius home. Hooray for Jesus! Hooray for Jesus!

I always knew that someday this would happen. I didn't know how or when but I knew it would because for years the doctors had been telling us all the things that could go wrong with Tavarius being in the condition that he is in. But it is hard to prepare yourself for something like this. I thought about it at times but I really didn't want to. And honestly speaking, I really didn't want to prepare for this because I didn't want it to happen, but it did.

They gave Tavarius another MRI and decided to keep him another week and try some different antibiotics. I was relieved that they were going to try something else instead of saying they had done all they could. It was better than them saying nothing was working and our only option was surgery. It gave me hope that they were going to try different medications and I counted on the medicine to get rid of the fluid and relieve the pain my son was experiencing. I wanted that to be the case, but deep down inside, I knew the day would come when surgery would be the only way to fix this problem and rid my son of this misery.

The doctors, their staff, and all the other hospital personnel were very nice and accommodating but we wanted our son at home. After staying in the hospital for seven days and nights they discharged Tavarius and gave us instructions regarding the antibiotics that he had been receiving. They also sent him home with some additional medication. They said that the current medication seemed to be working and at that point and time there was no need to discuss surgery. I'm sure I don't have to tell you how satisfied we were to hear that. It was difficult to watch our son experience the excruciating pain that he was dealing with day after day. If it wasn't the tendons in his legs it was his hips. And if it wasn't his hips it was the seizures. I just kept reminding myself that he was alive and that God would take care of him just like he had been doing. With all of the things that we have been up against, the thing that has kept us positive is our faith in God. Through Christ all things are possible—ALL things.

A few weeks after Tavarius came home things seemed to be going well. I counted the medication he was taking and at the time it was seven different types. Seven was quite a bit of medication for a child to be taking every day. More time passed and just when we thought we were in the clear with Tavarius' hips, they began to bother him again. We took him back to the clinic and they put him on some more medication for pain and inflammation. This whole thing with his hips started with one hip and then he just started having problems with them both. I mean we could actually see the bones sticking out. After going to the clinic and speaking with his orthopedic doctor, it was decided that the time had come for us to do what we dreaded the most. Tavarius had to have surgery.

I talked to Tavarius' teacher about the situation with him and his hips. She told me that she had met a gentleman whom was a Shriner and that she had already spoken with him about Tavarius and our book. She then educated me on the Shrine Organization and some of the things they do. I learned that they have hospitals all over the world. Even though Tavarius attended a Shrine school, I was under the impression that was where the generosity ended. I was blown away when she told me they help families like ours that have children like Tavarius. I even did some of my own research on the organization and was impressed with how incredible they were.

Other than the introduction given by Tavarius' teacher, this gentleman had no clue who I was. But he knew that Tavarius meant the world to his teacher and some of the other staff at his school. He wanted me to give him a call. I did as requested and gave him the history on Tavarius including how he was born a healthy child, but had been abused to the point of disability. As I explained some of the things Tavarius had been through, I had to say "hello" a couple of times to make sure he was still on the line. I'm sure he wasn't prepared to receive the information I had given him. After I finished giving him Tavarius' background, he told me more about their organization and the deeds they do for disabled children.

He wanted me to bring Tavarius to one of their Temples so that the doctor there could take a look at him to see if he would be a good candidate to visit one of their hospitals. He told me that if the doctor said Tavarius was a good candidate, they would send us to one of their hospitals for him to be evaluated. If everything with the evaluation went well they would do the surgery there at the hospital. He also told me that they would provide us with transportation and meals. The greatest news was that their organization would pay for the surgery, regardless of what type he had to have. I thought that was one of the most selfless and astounding things that someone could do for any child.

Again, I really didn't want to deal with the surgery but I knew that the time had finally arrived where that would be the only thing that would give Tavarius some relief from the unbearable pain he was experiencing daily. We prayed about it and said we would give it to God and that's exactly what we did.

Before Tavarius had the surgery we needed to make a decision about where it would be performed. We had to decide if the surgery would be done at the Shrine Hospital in St. Louis or Le Bonheur Hospital in Memphis. I had done some research on the Shriners hospital and I also wanted two different opinions. My wife felt like in a situation this serious we needed to weigh all of our options. So we decided to let the Shriners take him to their hospital for a complete evaluation. We would compare the information we got from them with the information we received from Le Bonheur and make our decision from there.

Tavarius and I took the six hour ride to St. Louis. We were accompanied by another child and his mother. They were actually on their third visit. Listening to her describe their experience with the hospital put me a little more at ease. I knew the decision was ultimately ours to make, but it helped to hear positive things about the hospital and the staff there. When we arrived at the hospital we had to go through pre-registration. Once the required paperwork was completed, it took about two hours for us to be seen by the team of doctors.

After the evaluation, the doctors basically told me the same things we had been told by Le Bonheur with the exception of one thing. But it was a big thing. They told me that while they could perform the surgery in their hospital, they would not be prepared if something went wrong like Tavarius having a seizure. I don't know if they told me that because of Tavarius' history with seizures or because a surgery of that magnitude could cause seizures. They told me that even though they weren't prepared that there were hospitals a couple of miles away and if something did go wrong it would only take a few minutes to get there. They weren't prepared for that because they were a hospital that specialized in orthopedic surgeries. I certainly appreciated their honesty, but they had definitely given me something to consider. I thought about what if during or after the surgery that Tavarius did have a seizure. They would probably need every minute to get the situation under control and may not have a couple of minutes to spare. Things really started going through my head like suppose they were transporting him to the other hospital and traffic got stalled. My mind was just full of what ifs. And none of those what ifs were chances and odds that I was comfortable with. The doctors understood my concerns and told me to go home and discuss it with my family and think about what we wanted to do. I kind of expected them to say go home and pray about it. I often wonder why doctors don't say that, especially in these types of situations.

My mind was actually made up once they told me they would not be prepared to handle the situation if Tavarius had a seizure. The fact of the matter was that as much as I didn't want it to happen, Tavarius had to have this surgery. I wasn't ready to sign off for him to have it but everything happens for a reason and sometimes we may not understand those reasons. On our journey back to Memphis, I pondered this surgery that we never wanted to talk about. I had to face the reality that the time had come and it needed to be done for our son's sake. I had close to six hours to let that soak in.

After we returned home from the hospital I anxiously waited for Gwen to come home so I could share with her what I had learned. I told her about our visit and what both sets of doctors had explained to me about doing the surgery on Tavarius and why it would be in his best interest. At that moment we both decided that the surgery would be the best thing for us to do in order to prevent our son from experiencing the pain he had been having for way too long. The next step was for us to get with Tavarius' orthopedic doctor and work out all of the details. Tavarius' doctor is very good at what he does. I just wasn't up for it because I still had not fully come to terms with Tavarius having the surgery. My biggest reason was that he had already been through so much and now we were getting ready to put him through more. We made the decision to have the surgery at LeBonheur instead of the Shriner's hospital. Thank God we did because Tavarius had a seizure during his recovery.

Before they took Tavarius into surgery, his doctor told us that someone would notify us every hour on the hour of how things were going with the surgery. He really moved us when he said he was going to treat Tavarius and the surgery as if it were his own son. Just the fact that he said that gave us all the confidence in the world in him. We actually were notified every hour on the hour just as he had assured us. The surgery lasted about three or four hours. The last call we received was to inform us that everything had gone well and that Tavarius was being taken to recovery and we could see him when they brought him down. Once Tavarius was moved to recovery we were right there. Gwen had to leave in order to be there when Demarian arrived home from school. I never left Tavarius' side and I am glad I didn't. I have also said that I wish maybe I hadn't been there to witness Tavarius having a seizure while he was in recovery. What I saw was so horrific that I immediately began to pray to God to please allow him to come through this ordeal without any further complications. It completely devastated me. It was like something out of a horror movie. Tavarius started throwing up some type of dark brown liquid. Not only was it coming out of his mouth, but it was coming through his nostrils as well. The ICU that Tavarius was in had about five or six other children so the nurses were pretty busy. No one even knew what was going on until I started yelling for help. Someone yelled out some sort of code and doctors and nurses started coming from everywhere. It was another horrific scene. They put tubes down his throat and his nostril all at the same time. I was so nervous I was a basket case.

I don't even like to think about what would have happened if we had decided to let the doctors in St. Louis perform the surgery and knowing they were not fully equipped to handle the situation when Tavarius was going through this ordeal. It took the team of doctors roughly five to ten minutes to get everything under control. I must have aged a couple of years during that short but scary time. I was so glad that Gwen wasn't there to witness what had happened. I know my wife, and they would have had to carry her out on a stretcher. When I spoke with her after she had gotten Demarian off his school bus, I told her not to worry about trying to return to the hospital because everything was okay. She would have also had to find someone to watch Demarian-so that was an easy fix. I did not tell my wife what happened to Tavarius while he was in recovery until later that night. We were talking on the phone and I filled her in on what had transpired that afternoon. I explained to her about the substance that was coming out of his body and then how the doctors came charging in as if Tavarius' life depended on them. She broke down crying on the phone. I reminded her that Tavarius was in the best care at one of the greatest hospitals in the state of Tennessee and in the hands of some of the greatest doctors. More important than anything, I reminded her that he was in God's hands. After Tavarius came out of recovery in ICU, they put him in a private room where he remained until they released him seven days later. We felt much better with him in that private room because we felt that meant he was out of the danger zone. If the doctors thought he was at risk for more complications they would have kept him in ICU where he could be constantly monitored. The staff continued to come into his room to check on him they were always caring and showed genuine concern. I realize that is their job, but there are some doctors and nurses who aren't so good at their job. They have horrible bedside manner, but I am grateful that wasn't the case for us.

There are scars on both of Tavarius' hips that are each about seven inches long. Tavarius was probably about three feet tall so those scars were very visible. The doctor and his team did a phenomenal job on his hips and we followed their instructions about how to care for Tavarius' wounds once he was released from the hospital and we took him home. It was during this time when we really had to come together and concentrate on doing what we had to do in order for our son to recover properly.

Thankfully, Tavarius' hips did heal properly. They flop but at least he is no longer in that excruciating pain that he had been dealing with. We were in a good place because Tavarius started back smiling all the time like he used to before his hips started getting the best of him. Having that taken care of released a lot of stress for us. Tavarius went back to school after being home for almost two months. He was a totally different child than he had been a few months before that. It was almost like night and day.

We did have to get him a new and different kind of mattress to sleep on because that is what the doctor recommended and we wanted him to be as comfortable as possible. The doctor gave us the specifics on the mattress and also told us that Tavarius' insurance would more than likely pay for it. I was glad because I know that some of those things can be very expensive. I mean we would have done whatever we needed to do, within reason, to get that mattress for Tavarius. But it was nice to know we were going to get some assistance. Having dealt with insurance companies in the past, I was prepared for their questions. I contacted the insurance company to tell them what Tavarius needed and why. They in turn asked me a million and one questions. I was prepared for a million questions but then they had to go and add that extra question. I am kidding. They did ask a lot of questions though, and their response didn't really make much sense to me. They said that even though the mattress was a medical necessity they could not pay for it. What they did offer though, was to pay for a medical bed. It wasn't what we were expecting, but we knew it would be good for Tavarius. The bed was much appreciated and to this day Tavarius continues to be pain free when it comes to his hips.

I have had a lot of great and wonderful moments with Tavarius. One of my greatest moments was when we went to the movies. The school that he attends often takes them on field trips and I go with them as often as I can. It is really amazing to see how a lot of these children enjoy themselves on the field trips. I will never forget how impressed I was when I found out the movie theatre we went to had closed the doors to the public just to accommodate these children. The majority of these children were in wheelchairs so they put them all down front on the floor except for the ones that could walk or use a walker. Those children were able to sit in the theatre seats. It was a wonderful feeling to be a part of their experience. Although Tavarius couldn't see, when those sounds erupted he screamed and laughed so hard that he actually brought tears to my eyes. I bought him a large hot dog and a large drink to wash it down with. That was a moment that I will remember for the rest of my life.

One year, before the Christmas holidays, the school took the children to Walmart so they could pick out something to take home. When Gwen and I first heard about it, we wondered how they were going to pull it off. They did. The school makes it a practice to take the children on outings, and they have the process down to a T. When we went to the movies there were 10-12 school buses, but when we went to Walmart they only took one class at a time. You should have seen us roll those children down the aisles in their wheelchairs. That was another proud and wonderful experience. Even though the children really couldn't tell us what they wanted, we treated them as though they could. They all left Walmart with something to take home. Another treasured moment that I will never forget.

Tavarius' school even took a trip to the mall for the children to see Santa. That was definitely an interesting trip. It was such a joy to hear the laughter and see the smiles on some of the children's faces. For Tavarius' school to take the time to do things like this for these children is such a heartfelt thing. Tavarius attends a Shrine school and I know the parents appreciate what they do for the children, I definitely appreciate it! All schools that have special needs children don't do the same things for their children that the Shrine school does. I do go on field trips with Demarian's school as well. And even though they don't have as many field trips as Tavarius's school does, they show just as much love.

Tavarius is getting older. I was talking to my wife about how much he has grown and how he has a mustache. I hope he doesn't start growing sideburns, or as some people like to call them, beards. At first it was him getting musty, then growing pubic hairs, now this. I guess we were only looking at his handicaps and not really thinking that a day would come where he would get older and his appearance would change. We were so busy thinking about the things we have to do for him that we weren't thinking about him getting older and the changes that would occur in both our lives and his as a result of that. When Tavarius was 16, sometimes at the end of the day, especially after his clothes had been removed and he was ready for a bath, he would be so musty that he smelled like onions. We actually started getting a whiff of that when he was 13. But that's a part of parenthood too, and that's what we have soap and water for.

There always seems to be never ending problems with Tavarius. It seems as though every few years he experiences some type of physical problems. What is so disturbing and heart breaking about it all is that Tavarius was born a healthy child. All of the problems that he has are a direct result of him being abused when he was an infant. I'm sure I sound like a broken record when I say that he is one of the reasons I am so adamant about putting this information out. Every time Tavarius has to go through a procedure or he experiences a difficulty, it takes me back to what happened to him and how it should have never happened.

Child abuse and Shaken Baby Syndrome have altered his life and he wouldn't have had the experiences he has if this hadn't happened to him. First, there is the fact that he is confined to a wheelchair for the rest of his life. Second, he is totally blind and has experienced multiple seizures during his 17 years. He had to have surgery on the tendons on the back of his legs because they were so tight and would not extend. And then there was the surgery on his hips. He had to have both of his hip bones shaved because they had come out of the socket so badly that it was breaking the skin on his hips.

Just recently we started dealing with another situation surrounding Tavarius' health. I had taken him to the doctor because I knew that something was going on with him but I couldn't pin point exactly what it was. He was coughing and rubbing at his ears, and he didn't have much of an appetite. From past experience, I knew that he was having either some throat or sinus issues. The doctor confirmed that he was dealing with a sinus infection and gave us a prescription for nasal spray and antibiotics. After about a week it seemed as though the infection was clearing up but he was still doing a lot of coughing. Since we knew he had allergies we figured that the cough would eventually go away, especially since sinus and allergy problems usually go hand in hand. After another week though, it appeared as though the coughing was getting worse instead of better. I told Gwen I felt like God was letting me know that we needed to take another trip to the doctor. I can always depend on God to give me that insight when it comes to dealing with the children and their ailments. Sometimes Gwen says I overreact when it comes to the children, but with them I just like to play it safe. When I went into Tavarius' room that morning I examined him closely as I do every morning. His shirt was soaked from sweat. I got a thermometer and put it under his arm and got a reading of 102.1. I knew then that I wasn't overreacting. That morning, Tavarius was headed to the clinic, and not to school. I literally hate taking the children to the clinic when they don't have an appointment. The wait is terrible and the fact that we were going on a Monday morning made it that much worse. One time I took Tavarius without an appointment and the wait was so ridiculous that I left and came back the next day. This time though, I was determined to stay until we had been seen.

I rolled Tavarius up to the front so that I could sign him in. As I was signing him in he started throwing up. When I saw what he was throwing up it seemed all too familiar to me. It was the same as the substance he vomited in the hospital after the surgery on his hips. Even though that's not what I wanted it to be, I had to be sure of what I saw. In the hospital it was a mixture of blood with anesthesia and other medications. The color was the same, but this time there was a lot of mucus as well. I was concerned, but wasn't feeling like it was the same thing because this time he had no anesthesia in his system. They immediately sent us to the back for the doctor to see him. She looked in his ears and noted that one of them was red, but she also wanted to take a look at his throat. She got the tongue depressor and as soon as she put it on his tongue he began heaving again.

There was a nurse in the room with us and I looked at her and the doctor trying to figure out what in the world was going on with my son. The doctor made a reference to coffee grinds and I didn't understand what she meant. That was her terminology for the dried blood that Tavarius had been throwing up. That scared me and I was trying to figure out how in the world my son was throwing up dried blood. Not only that, but why would he even have dried blood in his system like that. I had a lot of unanswered questions. The doctor told the nurse to call 911 so that Tavarius could be transported to the hospital. My nerves were wrecked and I had no idea what to expect.

When we got to the hospital they put him in a room and drew some blood for testing. After waiting for two hours they informed me that they were going to admit him. As nervous as I was, I was okay with them admitting him because I knew that something was wrong with him and we definitely needed to get to the bottom of it. They hooked him up to an IV and shortly after took him for an MRI and a few other tests. The doctor at the hospital confirmed that it was dried blood that Tavarius had thrown up. The doctor said he had an infected stomach along with a viral infection. I didn't know it then, but this was just the beginning of what was to come. They continued to give him test after test. Even though they knew it was dried blood at the bottom of his stomach and they knew he had an infection, what they did not know was why. They didn't know what was causing these problems.

We continued to see doctor after doctor with no answers. After two days of testing, they diagnosed Tavarius with a bulging hernia in his esophagus tube. I had never in my life heard of anything like that before. I have a bulging disc so I had heard of that before and knew what it was but a bulging hernia was something foreign to me. Especially in his esophagus tube.

Tavarius hadn't had much of an appetite since we arrived at the hospital so I decided to order him something to eat. He was on a regular diet and they hadn't given him any restrictions on what he could eat. After about his fourth spoonful everything came up. When the nurse relayed this information they decided to change his diet until they could run further tests. Later that evening, the nurse came back to administer his medication. As soon as she gave him the medication it came right back up. I was in panic mode, but the nurse called the doctor and explained to him what had just happened. The doctor ordered more tests for him, including a swallowing test. After getting all of the necessary tests done they determined that not only was there a problem with the hernia on his esophagus tube but that he needed a G-tube inserted in his stomach. That news threw me a curve ball. I was completely devastated.

After 17 years of being able to chew and swallow his foods without any problems or complications, within a matter of a few days, that all changed. This is not what we wanted but there was nothing we could do because he has to have food or some type of nourishment in his body. I prayed to the Lord and told him that I wasn't happy about it, but if it was his will, to let it be done. I have to trust Him because he has not failed us yet. It still didn't take away the fears that we had about him having that tube in his stomach. For some reason when I would see those children at his school with those tubes in their stomach, I almost felt like it was a death sentence. It's amazing what being educated about different things in life can do for your sanity. Initially all I could think about was our son having this hole in his stomach with this tube in it and it being a major problem.

We couldn't have been more wrong. Our son having this feeding tube was not as horrible and as complicated as we thought. Yes, it did alter his life as well as ours, but more than that it made him well, which is the most important thing. Tavarius had been taking some medication that I felt he shouldn't have been taking. It wasn't so much the medication itself, but the form is what bothered me. The medicine was in capsule form and from the very beginning Tavarius had difficulties swallowing them. After he started having issues with the hernia and the infections, I wondered if those capsules had been the culprit. I even asked the doctors about it and was very adamant about the possibility that the capsules could have caused his most recent problems. It bothered me for a very long time, but I did have a couple of conversations that put me a little more at ease about it. I have a cousin who is a doctor and he put my mind at ease a little. I also discovered that children with traumatic brain injuries like Tavarius, do have issues like this.

The morning that Tavarius was to have his surgery he had about five or six seizures back to back. That broke me and Gwen down. All we could do was pray to God to take care of our son while he was on that operating table. Tavarius stayed in the hospital 18 days and nights while they started a new chapter in his life and I was right there with him. The only time I left was a few hours on one day so that I could go home and cut my grass. Staying in that hospital was no picnic but it wasn't about me it was about my son and I would have stayed 18 more days if I had to. I just thank God that both the surgery with the hernia and the G-tube went well.

While I was at the hospital dealing with Tavarius' situation, my wife was home dealing with Demarian. She was having a very hard time with him. Every day that I spoke with her I could hear the exhaustion in her voice. Demarian was in school every day except the weekends, while Tavarius was in the hospital. Gwen would get Demarian ready for school and after putting him on the bus she would head to the hospital. The hospital definitely did not feed me all those days and nights and eating in the cafeteria got to be very expensive. I could always count on Gwen to bring me something to eat when she came for her visits. I don't know what I would do without her. But there were days that I told her not to even come to the hospital because I knew how exhausted she was dealing with Demarian and his behavioral problems.

One thing I learned while I was there at the hospital with my son is that when it comes to your loved ones, you have to be very vigilant. I remember one day Tavarius started having back to back seizures and for the life of me I could not understand what was going on. I later found out that someone had written down the wrong dosage of medication and they were not giving him enough. I was pissed! And you can believe that I let them know and that it was unacceptable. I also reminded them that a mistake like that could have cost someone their life. It didn't have to be my child, it could have been anyone's child. If that would have happened, it would have been too late to apologize. Once we went over the dosage of the medications he was supposed to be given, things went back to the way they were supposed to be. I don't even want to imagine what would have happened if I hadn't been there to address that issue because Tavarius cannot speak for himself.

We were so happy to get Tavarius home so that we could pamper and love him the way that we have always done and so that I could be home to help Gwen with Demarian. Before they let Tavarius come home, she and I had to take a class at the hospital so that we would know how to operate his feeding tube. Because of the feeding tube, we went from going to bed at 8:30pm to going to bed at 11:30pm. With the feeding tube, Tavarius has to be fed 5 times a day in four hour increments. It was very challenging in the beginning.

But even though Tavarius has to have five feedings every day of fluids going through a tube and a hole in his stomach, at least he is getting all the nourishment he needs at each feeding. Whatever nourishment he may have been missing when he was chewing and swallowing his food, he's not missing anymore. So in spite of it all, we continue to look at this as a blessing. There is still a possibility that the tube may not be a permanent thing. The doctors did tell us that after a few months we would have to bring Tavarius in for another test and if he does well then the tube could go away. There is still a chance that he could go back to chewing and swallowing his food like he has done in the past. But even if he doesn't we are prepared to accept the G-tube as being a part of his life. It is a blessing for him to even be alive after everything that he has gone through.

To add to that, because of Demarian's behavioral problems, he cannot be in the room when Tavarius is being fed. We weren't really expecting it to be an issue. However, one night we thought he was sleeping and Tavarius was on his last feeding. We heard a noise only to discover that it was Demarian playing with the pump. When Tavarius is feeding, the tube in his stomach is actually attached to the pump. We didn't even want to imagine what kind of damage would have been caused if that tube was yanked or snatched out of his stomach. So just to be on the safe side and keep watch on Demarian, I have the chore of sitting in a chair by their bedroom door until the feeding pump completely stops running.

Even though we have figured out how to handle the G-tube and his feedings, it didn't come without additional complications. The dosage of some of his medications have changed. He also urinates more frequently and his bowels appear to be running on a regular basis. These weren't issues that we were dealing with prior to the G-tube. Tavarius also sleeps a lot more than what we are used to and his seizure activity seems to be more frequent than normal. We did contact his doctor about this and they wanted us to bring him in for some testing. We have a few reasons for concern.

Tavarius went back to school after being out for about two months with the G-tube in his stomach. After being in school for about a week, something horrifying happened while we were at the barbershop one evening. Thankfully his nurse was with us. There is a part of the G-tube that is called a button. The nurse and my wife saw this button come out of his stomach and it sent us into a frenzy. When Tavarius was given the G-tube we had been told that it could come out. We were told a lot of them do, but we didn't prepare ourselves for that. We actually had an appointment at a clinic that was supposed to show us what to do when something like that happens and how to put the tube back in the proper way. That appointment was a month too late. Not only did the button coming out scare us to death, but we were ready to pick him up and get him to the hospital driving 100 mph. The nurse reminded us that we had time because it would take a little while before the hole started closing up. The thing about the G-tube is that if we would have waited even an hour before inserting that button back into his stomach, the hole would have closed up, he would have had to have surgery again, and that would have been a nightmare! We were told that as long as we insert the button back into its proper setting we didn't have to worry about the hole closing up. We thank God that he had a nurse and that she was there with us when that happened. We were so busy being confused and terrified to try to do anything. Everyone was shocked, everyone except the nurse. She sprang into action doing exactly what they paid her to do, take control of the situation. After she got the button back into Tavarius' stomach we took him home instead of to the emergency room. The nurse said there was no longer an urgent need to get him to the hospital because she had gotten the button back in. She said she would just call her agency to see if they had another button, just that simple. Or so we thought. We were just learning, and didn't know any better. The nurse went to Walgreens and another pharmacy to see if they had a button. She also went to one of our local hospitals to see if she could get one there. She informed us that the hospital told her she needed some type of authorization in order to purchase one. At the time I must have still been alarmed to follow along, but now that I think about it I am wondering why Walgreens would carry a G-tube button in their pharmacy. Now I did believe we should have been able to get one from the hospital though.

After none of those ideas panned out, I asked my wife to call Tavarius' other nurse and to see what she thought about the situation. Her response was that she thought we should take him to the hospital. That turned out to be the best thing. When we got to the hospital we explained to them what happened. The doctor told us that we had done the correct thing by bringing him into the hospital instead of the nurse trying to fix the situation. The doctor also explained to us that Tavarius' G-tube was fairly new and that it should be at least a year before anyone should try fixing the problem on their own if the tube were to come out again. He specified that the nurses were included in that because even though they knew what to do when the tube comes out, because of the wound being fresh, they don't want to take a chance on something going wrong. He was referring to us as well because we had not yet been educated on what to do if the tube were to come out again. They inserted a brand new tube and everything was fine. It took about ten minutes for us to be educated on the G-tube.

Along with the G-tube adjustment, we also have to make a decision about whether we are going to send Tavarius back to school or if we are going to home school him. There are things that need to be considered like the frequency and looseness of his bowel movements as well as the frequent urination. That could be a huge challenge when it comes to him attending school. Despite the obvious reasons, his school is also not equipped with the personnel that would be required to change him as frequently as they would now need to. With all of the special needs children that attend the school that would be a very difficult place to put them in. I'm sure that I could push the issue, but given the situation that's not something that I am willing to do. I think that would be selfish. At that point, it would appear that I would just be thinking about our situation and not the school or the other children that attend the school. If the school and their staff are not prepared for that then our child could end up staying wet longer or having poop on him longer than he should and that is not acceptable. We are also concerned that his seizures could once again become an issue. Even though right now I feel like we pretty much have them under control and they aren't one of my biggest concerns, the possibility is still there. But even with the other complications, they could end up changing his clothes four or five times a day.

Now don't get me wrong because we will do any and everything we have to legally to make sure that our sons get what they need. Anyone that knows us will tell you that when it comes to Tavarius and Demarian, the Stampleys do not play. We don't care who you are and what you represent because we represent those two unconditionally without a shadow of a doubt. At this particular moment we haven't made a decision about what we are going to do. Right now Tavarius has a nurse that is with him eight hours a day and that wasn't the case before his last hospital stay. We are definitely grateful for that. If we do end up home schooling him, all we would have to do is have the doctor draw up the necessary paper work and present it to the school. The amazing thing is that Tavarius' school already has teachers that do home schooling so the transition really wouldn't be that difficult.

Another wonderful thing about the homeschool situation is that right now, both Gwen and I are at home every day. Of course it would be a major change, but we would certainly welcome that change if it had to happen. At this point in our lives the most important thing is to make sure that the boys get what they need because unlike some other children, they definitely don't get what they want because they can't ask for anything. At this time, Tavarius is still attending school on what was supposed to be a trial basis to see how things would go. We had even considered doing half days if the situation warranted it. But so far, everything seems to be going well and we really plan to leave it like it is unless something else comes up. And if it does, we will cross that bridge just like we have every bridge that we have come up against.

DEMARIAN

Although I have not spoken about Demarian as much as I have Tavarius, we love and care for him the same. Demarian has tuberous sclerosis also called tuberous sclerosis complex (TSC). This is a rare genetic disease that causes benign tumors to grow in the brain and on other vital organs such as the heart, eyes, lungs, and skin. It usually affects the central nervous system and results in other issues including seizures, developmental delay, behavioral problems, skin abnormality and kidney disease. This disorder effects as many as 25,000 to 40,000 individuals in the United States and a million individuals worldwide, with an estimated prevalence of one in 6,000 newborns in all races and ethnic groups and in both genders.

I took Demarian to see his neurologist and it ended up being more of an adventure than either one of us anticipated. Unlike the visits we have for Tavarius, Demarian's visits usually only last between 45 minutes to an hour. That's not bad at all. This particular day his appointment was at 9:30am. Because the appointment was so early, I had planned on taking him to school after we left the doctor's office. The school allowed him to report to school tardy as long as he arrived before 11:00 am. Unfortunately two things prevented that from happening. The first was that we actually ended up being in the doctor's office much longer than we had planned. The first reason actually further aggravated the second reason.

As we were waiting, I got a whiff of an awful smell coming from Demarian. Although awful is actually putting it mildly. I quickly figured out that his bowels were running. Not good. He had actually been making the noises that usually signified that action, but I just thought he was clowning around—until the smell hit my nose. Fortunate for us, by the time the smell had escaped, we were in a patient room in the back of the clinic. I was almost expected to see something running down his legs. Quite often when we take the boys somewhere we dress them with two pampers. That day I hoped it would work out to my advantage.

I went to the front desk to find out if they knew how much longer the doctor would be. I explained to them our situation and that I didn't think we would last much longer. Thankfully, they informed me that the doctor was finishing up with the patient right before us and would be in shortly to see us. As we waited I prayed that the doctor would hurry up and make it to us before things really got out of hand. I could see a disaster about to take place. Graciously, God answered my prayer. The doctor entered the room only a couple of minutes later. As he examined Demarian I explained to him the dilemma we were having. Needless to say when the doctor got to Demarian's lower region his pants did not stay down long. But I did discover that the smell was worse than the actual damage. Yet and still, I was in a hurry to leave. Although I normally keep diapers in the car, I didn't bring any in with me because I assumed this visit would be short. The doctor had his nurses to check to see if they had any diapers but unfortunately they didn't have any to fit Demarian.

Once we left the doctor's office and were headed to the car, I felt a little relieved. We were no longer polluting the air and I felt like at that point if anything else happened we would be in the car. Worst case scenario, I would have to clean up the car and the car seat. But I hoped that would not be my fate. The ride home was breezy because we had to ride with the windows down. I appreciated the nice weather that day because had it been during the winter time, we would have been very cold.

Once we were home, I gave Demarian a bath and then fed him. A few hours later when Tavarius arrived home, the bus driver informed me that he had gone through two sets of clothing at school. He too, had running bowels. There appeared to have been a virus going around. Lucky us.

I took Demarian for a dentist appointment and saying that he cut up would be an understatement. He cut up sideways. It took three of us to hold him. Had we not been the ones brushing his teeth, I would never have known that one of them was loose. He surely couldn't tell us because even though he was seven at the time, he couldn't talk. That is why it is so important for us to pay attention and know what is going on with them.

One day we got a phone call from Demarian's school. They told Gwen that he had run into the corner of the black board and had a small gash in his head. He didn't have to have any stitches but his head was a little swollen. Demarian is always busy. We asked his doctor to consider medication to slow him down before he did some serious bodily damage. Sometimes at two and three in the morning, instead of being asleep, he would be up making noises and bumping his head.

After evaluating Demarian, his doctor agreed to put him on some medication for his behavior problem. From what we had been told, this medication was supposed to help him calm down. I remember some years back, one of his teachers warned me that as he got older, the behavior problem would get worse. He told the truth on that one. When we got the prescription filled for Demarian's medication we were able to see improvement in his behavior after about a week. He didn't get into things as much as he used to before taking the medication. Even his teacher at school said she could see a change in his behavior. Before, she would often tell me how he was always running around the room and trying to run out of the door whenever it was open. He did the same thing at home so I knew what she was referring to.

One day Demarian was sitting in his chair rubbing his eyes. But he had rubbed them so hard that he didn't even want us to touch him. When we tried to remove his hand from his eye he became so aggressive that he tried to kick us. I wondered what was really going on with him. My natural reaction was to just grab him and hold him as tight as I could. I had to remember that we were dealing with a child that had serious behavioral problems. It was only his left eye that he had rubbed. It took all the strength Gwen and I had to contain him and try to open his eye to see what was going on with him. After scuffling with him for a few minutes we were finally able to open his eye, but all we saw was redness. That really didn't help us. We knew something was very wrong. Even though he has behavioral problems, his behavior was extreme, even for him. The unfortunate thing was that Demarian couldn't tell us what was wrong if his life depended on it. He can't talk and has never been able to. I decided that I needed to take him to the doctor to get his eye checked out. Gwen and I figured that he had stuck himself in the eye with his finger. Sometimes he would stick his fingers in his nostrils and in his eyes. So that seemed like the logical answer. To be honest, I was surprised it hadn't happened prior to this time. When we got to the minor emergency clinic there were five children ahead of us. Just in case Demarian decided to get out of line, I informed the clerk at the desk that my child had special needs and that sometimes he would get excited—screaming and hollering. She let me know if that did happen, she had an area where she could seat us and it would just be the two of us there. That made me feel much better.

We had been sitting there for an hour and a half when a pregnant woman came in with her child and they called her to the back 30 minutes later. I was sympathetic about the pregnant mother being alone, not to mention the fact that she looked like she was actually about to have the baby. But my child was in some serious pain and I could not see where her child appeared to have any life threatening injuries. Despite my feelings, I decided not to speak on it. I tried to talk myself into not becoming angry and showing out. Just when I started to calm down, a couple came in with an infant child and they were called to the back about 15 minutes after arriving. At that point I was no longer able to keep my cool. I went to the desk and asked the procedures for being seen. The clerk explained to me that children are seen based on the severity of their illnesses and not necessarily on a first come first serve basis. Because I have repeatedly been to hospitals over and over with my children, I remembered that in my haste, I may have forgotten the process. I had to ask though. Shortly after me leaving the window, Demarian began to have one of his fits, screaming and yelling. The clerk remembered what she had promised and she did put us in a room that was in another area.

Finally, they called for Demarian. After the doctor came in and asked me what happened, I began with the explanation of Demarian's foster care and adoption history. I explained to her about his rare disease, Tuber-Sclerosis and how he had behavioral problems as a result of the disease. I trusted that she knew exactly what the disease was so that I wouldn't have to go into detail about it. It wouldn't have been a problem to do that, I just really wanted to get her to the point of how the disease was affecting him and why we were there. I explained some of his behavioral problems in detail and finally got to him sticking his fingers in his nostrils and his eyes, which I believed was our reason for being there.

She wanted to look into his eyes with her light to see if she could find out what was going on. I told her that it wasn't going to be an easy task. Demarian doesn't really like to be touched, especially by a doctor or anyone that looks like a doctor. I tried to explain to her how strong he was and how he wouldn't be a willing participant. I tried to warn her, but she had to find out on her own, just like everyone else who encounters Damarian for the first time. I knew what would happen once she and I tried to hold him and open his eye. Truth be told, I was already beyond frustrated just from waiting all day and I definitely didn't want to wrestle with this strong child. It didn't take her long to realize his strength. She tried to hold his head still and look in his eye at the same time. After he started kicking and swinging, she quickly put the brakes on and told me that she would be back with some help. That was more like it.

She left out of the room and came back with three other people—one was a female and the other two were guys that looked like they had been working out for a few years. That made five of us altogether. The doctor and the other lady, whom I assumed was a nurse, held his head, the other two guys held his arms and I tried to hold his legs. It took five of us to hold this little boy down just to put a couple of eye drops in his eye and during the whole ordeal they talked about how unbelievably strong he was. Maybe they were surprised, but I wasn't. I mean I had tried to warn her. I had these battles quite a few times, but no matter how many times, it never got easier. As a matter of fact, the older Demarian got, the stronger he got.

After the struggle was over and they were able to put the drops in his eyes. They determined that he had scratched the pupil in his eye. The doctor stated that it was a pretty long scratch and that he still needed to go to the hospital because he needed some type of special eye drops in his eyes. He also needed to be seen by an eye specialist, also known as an ophthalmologist, because if it wasn't treated properly the eye could become infected and that could cause him to go blind.

As we left the clinic and headed to the hospital, we were told that the hospital would be expecting us. Once we got to the hospital though, they said that no one had called them about us. Fortunately the waiting room wasn't very crowded and I had the paperwork showing that we had just left the clinic. They asked me the same questions that I had just answered at the clinic. I felt like a broken record, but I had done this enough times to know how it worked. So once again, I explained to the doctors in the room what had happened and how it was something that Demarian did at times. I also told them that my wife and I were really surprised that something like this hadn't already happened. I told them about his behavioral problems and how he would poke himself in the eye from time to time. They diagnosed him the same way they did at the clinic, but then the time came for those special eye drops. Damn! Here we go again. I tried to explain to them how difficult it would be to contain him and about the hard time we had just had at the clinic. They told me it wouldn't be a problem because they had something they could spray in his nostril that would put him out until they were able to check out his eye. As a matter of fact whatever they put in his nostril kept him out at least a good 30 minutes. What a relief that was! I know that anytime you are poked in the eye it is serious but this was mind blowing, I had no idea he had done that much damage.

The doctors at the hospital told me that they would make the necessary calls to get him where he needed to be so that he could get the best care possible. That following Monday we went to see the ophthalmologist and once again I had to repeat Demarian's life story and the whole chain of events. The ophthalmologist basically repeated everything that had been said to me both at the clinic and the hospital. Once again there were these special eye drops that Demarian needed and it seemed like we were in for another fight. The ophthalmologist didn't mention anything about magical nostril spray. We were able to get the drops in his eye and then we were given a prescription for some antibiotic eye drops that I had to put in his eye four times a day. On top of that I had to bring him in to see them every day for four days. That was one hell of a scratch.

The really sad thing about this situation surrounding Demarian poking himself in the eye is that there is really nothing that can be done about it. He is on all kinds of medication for his behavioral problems but there is no medication that will specifically stop him from poking himself in the eye or from sticking his fingers in his nostrils. We had already made an appointment with his neurologist about increasing his medication when the incident with his eye happened. Hopefully that incident would help to support our theory that his dosage needed to be increased. At the very least, we needed some type of plan to keep him from injuring himself.

One day my wife and I were headed out the door to run a few errands while the boys were at school and before we could make it out we received a call from Demarian's school. They had called to inform us that he had had a Grand Mal seizure and that they had just called 911 to have him transported to the hospital. Even though we were devastated to receive that news, we knew what was going on because we had been through it with Tavarius. If you've never seen a child have a Grand Mal seizure then thank your lucky stars. It is not something you want to see. When we arrived at the hospital we were on pins and needles because as I stated, those seizures are not pretty. We were at the hospital no more than 30 minutes and Demarian had another seizure. I pushed the help button for the nurses to come, but in my mind they weren't coming quick enough. I got the response I needed when I ran out into the hallway and yelled that my son was having another seizure. Even though Demarian had two Grand Mal seizures they both lasted about 30 seconds each. No seizures are good seizures but the less time they last the better the situation is. They told us that they would be sending us home with some medication called

Dias tat. They told us to follow up with his neurologist and that if he had any other seizures and they lasted five minutes or more to use the Dias tat, which was to be inserted into his rectum and supposed to stop the seizure. We weren't surprised that they sent us back home and we weren't surprised about the follow up or the medication because we had been down that road a few times before.

That medication was definitely helpful—for us and him. It didn't cure the problem but it definitely made a difference. Before he started taking the medication, he was more than a handful. He was still a handful, but he was more manageable. We would give him the medication before he went to school. By the evening time, though it would have worn off so he still wasn't really sleeping through the night. We thought it still may have needed to be increased just a tad more. Demarian had gotten more aggressive. So much so that he would try to hit at us. And the fact that he wasn't sleeping through the night was insane. I felt like Gwen and I would be taking nerve pills just to function and that wouldn't be good. Demarian is 12 years old and strong as an ox. I don't even want to think about the damage he'll be able to cause when he gets 14. We will probably have to start locking our bedroom doors and I refuse to become a prisoner in my own home. I have heard horror stories about children that have behavioral problems and some of the victims have died. We are definitely not trying to end up like that. I don't want our children, grandchildren, family members, and friends reading and hearing about how our son that we adopted, loved, and cared for bashed our heads in or stabbed us multiple times. I know that it sounds horrific but it is a harsh reality.

NEW CHAPTER

The Christmas holiday is especially hard for us. It should be a time for joy, but it is more sorrow. I say that because when we wrap gifts and toys for the children, there are no toys for Tavarius and Demarian because they can do nothing with them. We just buy them clothing to make sure they look nice. I would give anything to see these two children of ours enjoy toys and Christmas like normal children do. I probably should have gotten over it by now, but I honestly don't believe I ever will. Tavarius has been through 16 Christmases and Demarian has been through 12. Although neither one of them knows what that means or even recognizes that it's a special day, each year it continues to pain me. Even though I may not be around to see it, I pray that one day there will be cures for the ailments these children suffer with. They are denied the joys of childhood and that just doesn't seem fair. Despite their circumstances, they are happy children with healthy appetites, and are truly a blessing to us.

NEW CHAPTER

A couple that we considered friends was getting married and instead of asking someone from either of their families, they asked us if Tavarius could be their ring bearer. Of course, we said yes. So Saturday, September 20 was a very busy and special day for us. We were very excited to see our friends get married and it meant even more to us that they thought enough of us and our son to want him in their wedding. That was an event we will cherish for the rest of our lives.

Because of our involvement in the wedding, our otherwise normal routine was anything but normal on this day. Gwen had to do some of the cooking for the wedding so I was responsible for taking care of the boys and transporting the food. We were supposed to be at the location at 630p so after we got dressed, we worked on the boys an hour and a half ahead of time. We arrived exactly at the time we were expected. Even though Demarian wasn't in the wedding, we dressed him as though he was. We couldn't put Tavarius in a suit and not have one for Demarian as well. They both looked very dapper.

The wedding took place in a backyard. I had never been to an outdoor wedding but the atmosphere and decorations were beautiful. Because Tavarius was the ring bearer and was unable to hold the rings in his hand, we had to put them in his shirt pocket. I wanted to put them in his coat pocket, but while getting him dressed, I noticed he didn't have one. Since I was in the wedding as well and would be standing next to him, I actually held on to the rings. But when the preacher asked for them I pretended to remove them from Tavarius' shirt pocket.

Everything went perfectly and we partied until late that night. Tavarius is a huge fan of music and there was both a live band and a DJ. He was moving so much that he was bucking his wheelchair. He had a ball. The only time he didn't move was when there was slow music playing, but the minute the beat changed, he was back to moving again. It was a joyous sight to see. Even though Tavarius is disabled, he recognizes music and has plenty of soul.

Unfortunately during the ceremony, Demarian wasn't as easy going as Tavarius. There were four or five us that took turns watching him throughout the night. He is not wheelchair bound like Tavarius and there was so much excitement that he could hardly contain himself. We all had a ball. In fact, so much so that the next morning we didn't even get out of bed until 9:00am which was extremely late for us. We actually could have stayed in bed a little longer but the boys are our number one priority and no matter how tired we are, they have to be fed and medicated. We did lounge as much as possible though between those routines. Later that evening Gwen cooked her huge Sunday dinner as she usually does, and we went back into relaxation mode.

We all had a great time and it brings us such joy to know that the boys really enjoy themselves and we can tell. A few years ago, we contacted the Make-A-Wish Foundation. We finally received a response from them and they informed us that the foundation had granted our children an all-expense paid vacation to Disney World in Orlando, Florida. If you are not aware of the organization, it is a non-profit organization that grants wishes to families that have a child or children with life threatening illnesses. The trip was for six days and nights. We lodged on their property and it was like a community with houses that were very well kept and yards that were very well groomed. The houses were equipped with washers and dryers and even had Jacuzzis. They also had full kitchens and flat screen televisions. Out on the property site was a swimming pool, a water park, cartoon characters, and a dining area where you could get three meals a day along with terrific and awesome volunteers. There was also an ice cream parlor on the property that stayed open all night. Walmart was about 2 miles from the property and they even had a shuttle service to take you there and back. There was free pizza delivery and a place where you could get sandwiches, cookies, chips and other snacks when the dining area was closed.

I'm sure you can tell that we were just as excited and had just as much fun as the boys did. I ate banana splits four of the six nights that we were there. I even had chocolate chip cookies a couple of nights. Even though I am a diabetic, you only live once and that was definitely a once in a lifetime opportunity.

One of the things I wanted for the boys to experience was a live pony ride. Even if they didn't get to actually ride, but at least sit on the pony. With the help of the wonderful people at Disneyworld we were able to do just that. We got the opportunity to attend a couple of parades on the property and we even went on a safari that reminded me of one of those Tarzan movies. We were literally within a few feet of those animals. People were actually speculating what we would do if something happened like the jeep stopping or the animals going insane. Gwen and I were looking at each other like, "what are we doing?" Reality settled in for a few minutes. I mean I'm sure they had taken all the necessary precautions to make sure none of that would happen and they know that they are responsible for people's lives but we just couldn't help thinking "what if?" We saw lions, tigers, hippos, giraffes, and even alligators. All animals that appeared to be in their natural element. Even if we had to run, we have a teenage son that can't even walk, much less run. Our other son can do both, but sometimes he doesn't want to do either. I could just imagine us trying to run and hide at our age—me running with Tavarius in my arms and trying to pull Gwen and Demarian to who knows where. Just thinking about the outcome of that situation gave me chills. Again, I know that they try to take all of the necessary precautions, but sometimes things happen. You have airplanes that go down, and people getting stuck on rides 200 and 300 feet in the air. I know the chances are slim, but it doesn't stop my mind from wandering.

But back in the happy place outside of my thoughts, Disneyworld had a carousel that children in wheelchairs could ride without them being taken out of their wheelchairs. We had never seen anything like that and we were so excited.

That was a trip that my wife and I will remember for the rest of our lives. While we sincerely appreciated the trip and we all enjoyed ourselves tremendously, there were times when we were completely exhausted just from the boys and their excitement. Demarian was overly anxious and did not make it easy on us at all. He cut up terribly. Tavarius is confined to a wheelchair on a daily basis, but during our visits to the different sites and parks we actually had to rent a wheelchair to push Demarian in because he didn't want to walk. As we went around the properties, he would occasionally fall down on the ground because he didn't want to walk. Initially we thought it was because he was in a new surrounding and hadn't gotten adjusted yet. As time went on though, we realized he was just being himself and being stubborn. Although Demarian has tumors on his brain and is mentally challenged, he does understand some things that he does, like falling out and not wanting to walk. So instead of pushing one wheelchair, we ended up pushing two. That sounds like it would have been easier but even though Demarian was in the wheelchair he just cried and hollered to the point that sometimes people were just staring at us. I wasn't concerned about the people looking, I just wanted him to calm down. By the time we got home, we needed another vacation by ourselves. The trip was eventful and we were so thankful for the opportunity. But we decided that even if they were to offer us another trip, we would not take it. Demarian was such a handful that he wore us down more than usual.

NEW CHAPTER

While attending one of my grandson's football games, I ran into a young lady that I knew. We spoke about my book and she told me about her personal situation. She had left her child in the care of one of her family members and that family member abused her child. She said that because the state felt that she was responsible, they removed her other children from the home. If her account of the story was accurate, then she wasn't being treated fairly. That was wrong—the mother knows, you and I know, and the state knows! She went on to say that the state eventually found out who the culprit was. They took her through hell and high water for two years about her children, only to apologize for what they had done. How can you remove someone's child from their home because they left them with someone that they trusted? It wasn't her fault that a family member abused her child. That time I was on the parent's side, not because I know her, but because what was done to her was wrong. As I've said, each case is different. Some parents get a bad rap even though they are being mistreated. But it boils down to people doing their jobs and being held accountable.

From time to time I still read where children have died and could have been saved if certain individuals had done their jobs while these children were still in the system. As a matter of fact, I remember that there were different news media that sued the Department of Children Services (DCS) because they were hiding records of the children that had died or were seriously injured while they were in DCS custody. For years officials have refused to comment about abuse cases or neglect due to confidentiality. *"What is known came from heavily redacted files that news organizations obtained under public records requests and by court order. Those requests centered on information about 200 DCS investigations of children who died or were seriously injured between 2009 and 2012."*[1]

In one case a three-year old girl was abused and nearly overdosed on pain killers during a trial home visit with her grandmother. In another

---

[1] Lollar, Travis. "DCS Records Unclean in Child Death." *Commercial Appeal* [Memphis] 10 Feb. 2013: n. pag. Print.

case a fifteen year old boy who was supposed to be in DCS custody, died after a car accident with his drug intoxicated uncle behind the wheel. The teen had gone missing two months before the accident. There was nothing in the records that showed DCS had made an effort to find him. In yet another case, an 11-month old baby living with his mom in a shelter for victims of domestic violence was found dead. The cause of death wasn't determined although the boy had previously been sick with pneumonia. It was the third time DCS had been called about the family in a 5 month period. The mother moved to Kentucky and DCS closed the case.[2]

In October 2010 a 9-month old baby was brought to the hospital with severe head injuries. DCS was not in touch with the family prior to the baby's injury. The baby died and DCS took her surviving sister into state custody, placing her with relatives.[3]

And then in yet another case the same month, an 8-year old boy suffering from asthma, cardiac problems and seizures was sent from school to the hospital in an ambulance. The case worker found the parents were medically neglecting the child. DCS had been called in before on similar allegations. The boy and his sibling were left with their family.[4]

These cases only came to the forefront because of the continued and aggressive efforts that the media pursued to make this information available to the public. None of these things should have ever taken place. The fact that the media had to file a lawsuit against DCS to get this information is a total disgrace. As long as there are individuals not doing their jobs like they should be and covering up these abuse cases, we will continue to have children being abused and dying. I almost feel like the case number has to reach the millions before they start making drastic changes. It's already in the thousands. Or maybe, it will have to hit closer to home.

There was an article published by our local newspaper October 8, 2012. The article stated that the Department of Children Services and its Commissioner had been under fire the past few weeks after complaints that the department was not properly intervening in cases where children might

---

[2]   Lollar, Travis. "DCS Records Unclean in Child Death." *Commercial Appeal* [Memphis] 10 Feb. 2013: n. pag. Print.

[3]   Lollar, Travis. "DCS Records Unclean in Child Death." *Commercial Appeal* [Memphis] 10 Feb. 2013: n. pag. Print.

[4]   Lollar, Travis. "DCS Records Unclean in Child Death." *Commercial Appeal* [Memphis] 10 Feb. 2013: n. pag. Print.

be at risk. They were also under fire for violating a state law that requires the agency to report to lawmakers each death of a child under investigation.

"The situation did not attract much attention on the side of the state, but it raised important questions about accountability and transparency in protecting the safety of children in state custody. There is no room for lapses in these standards."

"The heightened scrutiny came after news reports that DCS said 10 infants whose cases were under active investigation were among 31 deaths of children in 2012 investigated by the department. Among the deaths, according to the reports, there were a total of 17 children whose care had been investigated by DCS. In 2012 alone, there were four children who were in state custody that died."

"The governor called the 31 deaths distressing, but said there was no immediate evidence of wrongdoing by DCS. Meanwhile, it was stated that cases were being reviewed on how severe child abuse cases were being handled and that the agency would work closer with child advocacy centers across the state to make sure severely abused children were not being overlooked by the state. That was a good start, but the public has to wonder why this had not been the norm."

Child abuse is a serious problem nationwide. "No child deserves to suffer injury or death at the hands of an abusive or negligent adult. DCS is there to protect at-risk children-to place them in homes where they will find nurturing and safety. But the agency's job doesn't stop there. There must be sufficient follow-up to make sure those children are receiving proper care and to intervene when there are signs that children's safety and welfare appear in jeopardy."

"It is incumbent upon the governor and the General Assembly, in this era of state budget cuts, to make sure DCS has the staff for that. And the commissioner needs to impress upon her staff the importance of transparency and proper reporting. It is easy to lose the trust and confidence of legislators and the public if the department nourishes a perception that DCS operates behind a veil of secrecy."[5]

Although these words are not mine and were printed in the local newspaper, I certainly agree with everything that was stated. These are some of the same issues that I wrote about in my first book and I still feel

---

5   "At Risk Children Must Be Protected." *Commercial Appeal* [Memphis] 8 Oct. 2012: n. pag. Print.

as though they are not being heard. Now that some of this information has been released by the media I wonder if it will still fall on deaf ears or will there actually be work done towards making a difference. Based on my past experience, I can't say I think it is the latter. I would like to feel differently, but I can't because I have yet to see any changes being made. There is talk about changes being made, but nothing is being implemented or enforced. The same things that were going on 17 years ago when we got Tavarius from the system, are the same things that are going on now. If that wasn't the case then the local newspaper wouldn't have been so adamant about filing a lawsuit to bring information to light.

Yesterday a 10-month old infant died from abuse. It was later determined that she had been hit in the head with a set of dumb bells. Another senseless killing of one of our innocent babies. How in the hell does someone hit a baby in the head with a set of dumb bells? That person couldn't have any brains and in my opinion should have been in a mental facility a long time ago. I don't know what it is going to take but we must all come together and come up with some type of plan. The infant was killed at the hands of a 16-year old.

From January 2008 to October 2008, there were 12 children murdered, and that is just in Memphis. Sadly, all of those deaths were committed by adults. In order to stop the senseless killings, the laws must get tougher. Somehow the judicial system is not sending the right message. In my opinion, if someone kills a child and that death is the result of any form of abuse, then that person should be incarcerated or institutionalized for the rest of their days. Maybe it won't stop the killings altogether, but those consequences would definitely make people think differently before doing something as inhumane as taking a child's life. One murdered child is one too many.

It really hurts my heart when I think about how violence has ruined Tavarius and other children like him. I used wonder what was going on in the minds of the offenders when they commited these violent and horrific crimes. I certainly don't have the answers and don't think there are many that do. It hasn't always been like this. Although there may have been some isolated cases in the past, it is definitely getting worse and becoming more commonplace. Every time I hear about a child that has been abused, I get sick in the pit of my stomach. It makes it worse when I hear that the abuser is a family member. I'm sure the thought process for a lot of these offenders is that they won't get caught. But eventually they will have to pay for their crimes, if not by man, definitely a higher power.

There are a few reasons that it is so important to address this issue of abuse. First, because it's the right thing to do. Second, because a lot of people that are abused end up abusing others. And third, in order to combat this terrible issue, help must also be made available for the people that commit these horrific crimes. I will be one of the first to say that a person that commits crimes like these against our beautiful, defenseless children should be punished to the maximum. I do understand though, that if these individuals don't get the proper help that they will probably repeat the crimes that were done to them.

There are people that want children and for whatever reason, cannot conceive them. And yet there are people that have children and are destroying their lives. I have often said and my feelings remain the same, that when these types of crimes are committed, the perpetrator should be locked up for a very long time. I don't consider ten or even 15 years to be a long time. If you destroy a child's life because of violence then your life should be destroyed. If someone cripples a child, then their life should be crippled by giving them 30 or 40 years without parole. If a child dies from violence, then that person should be incarcerated for the rest of their life. I make no apologies for where I stand on that. I feel this pain every day when I look at my children. Tavarius' conditions come from being abused and although as far as we know Damarian wasn't physically abused, he was neglected which deteriorated his ailments.

In 2008, we got a new President; the first African American President this nation has had. With his installment into office, I was hoping and praying for new social changes-specifically relating to our special needs children and the children that are in the foster care system. There are so many changes that need to be made when it comes to the welfare of these children. Between the violence in the streets, and the neglect, abuse, and murder of these children, I sometimes wonder how much of the next generation of children will actually be around. I have some contacts that work within the juvenile system and they agree that many things which should have changed have still not been addressed. We even spoke with one of the siblings of one of our sons and were told that some of his siblings are still in states' custody. Our son has been with us more than five years. It is painful to know that some of those children are still in foster care.

A child with special needs was left on one of the buses in freezing temperatures. This child was five years old. If the child had been a normal five year old, I'm sure he/she would have been able to let someone know that he was still on the bus, but he wasn't able to. My understanding is that the child was picked up when school was dismissed at 3:30pm and was not found until 5:30pm.

We would like to see a law passed that states that children stay in foster care for a certain length of time and when that time expires they can be adopted, especially when there is someone that wants them. We need this to be a firm law, so that children will not have to stay in foster care as long as Tavarius and Demarian did. There is such a law, but it is not enforced the way it should be.

There are other laws that need to be changed when it comes to these children that are stuck in the system. When a child is removed from their home because of abuse and/or neglect, the state should not have to wait and get consent from the parents to provide the child with services they need.

This is just prolonging the situation. Prolonging services the children need because the parents are not cooperating isn't helping these children.

I learned from a reliable source that the Department of Children Services was still up to their same tricks. I was told there was a little girl in foster care that needed some services done and because her birth mother was not cooperating, she would not be able to receive those services. You shouldn't always believe what you hear, but I believe this because my source is reliable and because I know how twisted the system can be.

There should already be a law in place that states that if a child or children are in states' custody and the child needs some type of services that are beneficial to them, the parents have a certain amount of time to respond. If the parent is being contacted regarding services then they should only be allowed a certain amount of time to respond. Maybe a week is reasonable, but in the case of emergencies, they should only be given 24-48 hours, depending on the severity of the situation. Contacting the parents should merely be a courtesy. If they don't get a response within that required timeframe the services should still be rendered to that child.

NEW CHAPTER

When I first wrote about our medically fragile children, I sincerely wanted to make a difference, especially after I found out how much I felt like the system was failing not only our children, but our society. We have encountered so much negativity that it saddens me every time I think about it. Even sometimes from the media to politicians. I wrote my first book because I was determined to let people and society know that there were things going on within the system that desperately needed to be addressed. We still have children that are getting lost in the system and even others who are dying.

I have come up with an idea that I think would help address this issue. I see nothing wrong with implementing something into all of the school systems. A safety measure that could be added to the school's curriculum. That safety measure would deal with child safety, child abuse and neglect, as well as Shaken Baby Syndrome. As we know, but a lot of times ignore, there are an alarming number of pregnancies that occur each and every year to underage teenage girls. The majority of teenagers, both male and female have no clue about babies, or Shaken Baby Syndrome. If I were a betting man, I would say that if you were to ask 20 teenagers between the ages of 13 and 17 if they know what Shaken Baby Syndrome is and the devastation that it causes to an infant's life, I bet you 15 of them would not know and that is because no one really talks about it, even though they really should. It is something that occurs every day and precious lives are lost because of it. I am not saying that putting this information in the school system would eliminate the problem, but it would sure as hell bring attention to and educate our children about the safety and caring of these babies being brought into the world.

Not only would this educate our children, it would also educate a lot of our adults. Surprisingly, there are just as many adults that are not educated about Shaken Baby Syndrome as there are teenagers. I really believe that implementing this education into the school systems would address the problem on a national level and it would affect so many lives. If this education is implemented, the children should receive a credit towards their grades and they would also become educated about the safety and protection of innocent babies. This puts them in a win-win situation by receiving additional credit and learning lifetime skills. Again, I know this will not solve the problem, but we have to come up with a plan to combat this problem early on.

To be honest with you, I sometimes wonder if the individuals who are in a position to do something about this, actually give a damn. My thoughts are not based on assumptions. I have brought certain things to the attention of people that I know are in a position of power and my concerns seem to fall on deaf ears. I am learning that it is really about the people who are making the decisions and not the children themselves. $124 billion dollars annually is a yacht full of money. That's how much money is spent on child abuse each year.

Like I said, implementing this curriculum into the school system won't solve the problem but it could definitely save lives and put a huge hole in $124 billion. I just don't think enough is really being done to combat abuse. America spends billions of dollars fighting wars and sending people into space, but can't come up with solid programs for educating people on child abuse! Give me a break! I understand that wars must be fought and that political progress must be made. But what about the progress of the children that never reach their peak because some sick individual decided to destroy their lives.

When I joined Facebook a few years back, it was because one of my daughters brought to my attention the fact that I could promote not only my book, but awareness about abused and neglected children and how they were getting lost in the system. I actually started sharing the information on Myspace and after a couple of years I moved on to Facebook. My sole purpose was to put the information out there. But both of those sites are social media outlets for anyone who wants to participate. What I learned and accepted are that just because there were issues that needed to be desperately addressed about our children and their future, doesn't mean every one shared my thoughts or disgust in the situation. At times I became frustrated because I was thinking about all of the abuse and deaths surrounding these children every day, yet it seemed that a lot of people continued to ignore what was going on. But then I reminded myself that if only one person pays attention to what is happening and they act on it then my work is not in vain. It may not touch all the people I want, but some awareness is better than no awareness at all.

You can't make the right decisions about these children's lives with just paperwork. You have to be actively involved and be an advocate for these children. They are helpless and we as a society must keep fighting for them until the necessary changes are made. A chain is only as strong as its links, so we must continue to make these links strong until we have locked this thing down. Awareness is our key.

You and I as a society can no longer sit back and witness things that are wrong and things that are being done wrong when it comes to our children. We must take a stand. We are not talking about a small crime like stealing a bag of chips, we are talking about child abuse-a serious, life threatening crime.

When we talk about abuse of these children, it's not just physical abuse or neglect. There is also sexual abuse. As I continue to try to understand why so much abuse happens to our children, I am consistently educated about how some individuals that have committed some of these horrific crimes were at some point in their lives abused themselves. But that does not excuse them for what they do. I have participated in discussions with individuals of different professions and even a couple of them that have been abused. After listening to these individuals, I have also learned that although a lot of the abuse occurred years ago, some of them are still not willing to talk about it. Some of them even feel that it is their fault and then some of them did come forward but nothing happened.

I am to the point that I have become so frustrated with the politics and red tape that myself and other caring individuals have to deal with when it comes to the safety of our children. I used to get upset quite a bit, but I learned the hard way that I had to turn that rage into something positive, like writing two books. I express myself and try to turn the negative into positive. I don't really know if I am making a difference by telling my story and trying to educate people about the system and abuse that occurs, but what I do know is that God has called me to speak up about what is happening to his innocent babies. I continuously do that to anyone who will listen.

I know that there is a God and we believe in Him. We just wonder sometimes with all that our children go through how much more pain will they have to endure in their lifetime. No one but God knows what the future holds but whatever it holds I sure hope and pray that whatever other task that is ahead with our two sons that God will continue to supply our every need and continue to make sure that we keep our sanity.

ABOUT THE AUTHOR

My name is Henry Stampley, I am 63 years old. I was born in Vallejo California and now reside in Memphis, Tennessee with my beautiful wife Gwendolyn and our two special needs sons whom we adopted. My wife and I have been married for 27 years. Together we have 7 children with the addition of our adopted sons. We also have 10 grandchildren. My wife and I were foster parents for a number of years before we adopted our 2 sons. We have had a total of 6 foster children that we have cared for over the years. One of the greatest joys from the experience of being a foster parent was the adoption of our sons. Our oldest son Tavarius inspired me to write my first book A Fragile Child's Cry and it is because of both of my sons that I decided to do my second book which is titled 17 years and still struggling.

Printed in the United States
By Bookmasters